How

to Be a

Hepburn

in a Hilton

World

How

to Be a

Hepburn

in a Hilton

World

The Art of Living with Style,
Class, and Grace

JORDAN CHRISTY

CENTER
STREET®

NEW YORK BOSTON NASHVILLE

Center Street

Hachette Book Group

237 Park Avenue

New York, NY 10017

Visit our Web site at www.centerstreet.com.

Center Street is a division of Hachette Book Group, Inc.

The Center Street name and logo are trademarks of Hachette Book Group, Inc.

Printed in the United States of America

First Edition: August 2009

10   9   8   7   6   5   4   3

Library of Congress Cataloging-in-Publication Data

Christy, Jordan.

How to be a Hepburn in a Hilton world : the art of living with style, class, and grace / Jordan Christy.—1st ed.

p. cm.

ISBN 978-1-59995-183-6

1. Young women—Conduct of life.   2. Etiquette for young women.
3. Charm.   4. Fashion.   I. Title.

BJ1681.C47 2009

170.84'22—dc22

2008053769

Contents

How

to Be a

Hepburn

in a Hilton

World

Stupid Girls

"Girls can be stupid." —*Becky Christy*

It would be naive to think we could ever again have a woman exactly identical to Jackie O., Audrey Hepburn, or Mother Teresa; we live in a different world now, and like my mom says, "It was a simpler time then." We don't typically gather the family around the transistor radio anymore or get asked to go steady by a Wally Cleaver, but just because we're surrounded by BlackBerrys, miniskirts, and *The Real World* doesn't mean we can't take some of those graceful, sophisticated, old-fashioned values and implement them in our everyday, modern-girl lives. Let's be honest: our current female landscape is embarrassing, flippant, and shallow. We need to start representing a new type of It Girl—a successful, stylish, smart girl who still maintains classic ideals and values. Is that possible, you ask? Yes. Yes! YES!

My mother is a very wise, beautiful, and funny woman. Over the years, she has taught my sister and me invaluable life lessons and passed along nuggets of wisdom, such as, "Don't stick any knives in the toaster while I'm gone." One of her most comical and ingenious statements came a few years back when I was home from college, rambling about how I had found there were very few girls I actually wanted to hang out with—it seemed to me that, in general, the majority of our gender were capable of only superficial attitudes, boy-obsessed rants, and dumbed-down speech. In response to my tirade, she accurately and simply summed up my sentiments, saying, "Well, girls can be stupid."

I think it's safe to say we all know a Stupid Girl or two. They're tossing their hair by the water cooler at the office, they're sporting silky thongs with low-rise pants in the grocery line, and there's at least one in every good reality show. They crash their BMWs in Hollywood, excessively use the word *like*, and drape themselves all over the nearest male. They're obnoxious and, for some reason, always the center of attention. Why? Because smart, classy, and successful ladies' slots on the local news have been supplanted by a play-by-play of Paris's clinkworthy antics and Lindsay Lohan's spiral into rehab. Even when the limelight finally shifts away from one Stupid Girl it only shines on another one who is all too willing to sell her self-respect for a little "free" publicity. Our girl-world has become saturated with fishnet hose and unflattering f-bombs, and thanks to the vicious media cycle of contagious celebrity gossip and endless barrage of Girls Gone Wild horror stories, it appears as though the majority of our female generation is being represented by a couple of skinny airheads out in LA.

I think we can agree that while most of us don't even begin to consider those girls to be accurate representations of our kind, much less role models, it is somewhat vexing that they dominate the headlines day in and day out. Clearly, scandals sell, and these girls certainly provide more than enough fodder for news outlets, so while they may not have one valid exploit or commendable achievement to claim, they are definitely making someone a whole lot of money. Before the Stupids came to power, gossip rags had to resort to "Four-Headed Alien Baby" and "Polka-Dotted UFO Sighting" headlines, but these girls have eliminated the need for fabricated news—their exploits are ridiculous enough to sell millions of glossy tabloids every week! And thanks to our culture's reality-TV-induced obsession with drama and incessant need for water-cooler small talk, we continue to put these girls in the spotlight by engaging in the round-and-round cycle of celebrity gossip and constant enthrallment with shallow, scandalous news. Even if we balk at their actions and roll our eyes at their lewd behavior, the ad dollars keep cha-chinging while their scandalous outings keep them in our faces 24/7. It's hard not to participate in discourse about their conduct, but if we want to begin cultivating a culture of class, style, and grace, we'll have to stop focusing on the Stupid Girl captions and start making our own Smart Girl headlines.

There's no getting around it, my mom was absolutely right: girls can be stupid. Pink's commentary on this current mindless epidemic in her hit song "Stupid Girls" is all too perfect. She has said in response to the controversy over the video, in which she portrays celebrities such as Jessica Simpson, Mary-Kate and Ashley Olsen, Lindsay Lohan, and Paris Hilton doing everything from shopping and tanning to awaiting cosmetic surgery and just being painfully thin, "Smart and sexy are not oil and water," and she explains the song title: "My definition of stupid is wasting your opportunity to be yourself." So many girls are indeed wasting their opportunity. We live in a free country with rights, freedoms, and opportunities that women would have killed for a hundred years ago—and instead of voting, getting the CEO spot, going for a doctorate, or volunteering at a women's shelter, many young women today are too busy shaking their badonkadonks in short-lived music videos and diligently bedazzling their cell phones with more pink rhinestones.

Even more sadly, our society has placed girls like this on a reality-television pedestal and kicked classy and well-spoken ladies to the curb. Think about it. Have you ever heard of Nancy Alcorn and her international organization that freely houses thousands of at-risk females? Or Cathleen Black, the "First Lady of American Magazines" and one of *Forbes*'s 100 Most Powerful Women? What about Sarah Ratty's ground-breaking eco-conscious clothing line, Ciel? Of course not! Let's face it—it's high time some extraordinary young women brought self-respect, intelligence, and true beauty back to the female gender.

Do you remember your first encounter with a Stupid Girl? Ah, what an unforgettable moment. The first Stupid Girls I recall meeting were Mandy and Heidi in my seventh-grade class (names have been changed to protect the ignorant). When they weren't busy making out with the better half of the JV basketball team, they would start malicious rumors, rip off the smart kids' essays, and periodically banish core members from their exclusive clique—all while proudly displaying their junior high goods in the tightest Abercrombie shirts money could buy. Their demure and tactful sides would particularly shine through during any event or rally that required the ascent of bleachers, and I specifically remember hearing about the classiness of the weekend that they discovered Pabst Blue Ribbon. They were your classic Stupid Girls.

Now, I was perfectly content flipping through Delia's catalogs, listening to Bruce Hornsby and *The Joshua Tree*, and writing amateur pop songs on my keyboard after school every day, so I never really got the appeal of the Stupid Girls. I remember noting all of their antics with mild amusement and silently wondering what on earth they would turn out like as adults, but I can't honestly say that their whole shtick appealed to me. In fact, it actually revolted me more than anything and eventually became my catalyst for trying to represent a different type of young female—a successful, smart, stylish girl who didn't give away all her dignity. When given the choice to go out boozing or stay home and watch *Steel Magnolias* with my mom and sister, I always opted for the latter. If I had the choice between dinner and good conversation with my best friends or hitting the party circuit to meet up with less-than-desirable high school males, I would end up splitting a pizza every time. I discovered that I didn't have to participate in the Stupid Girls' cruising-the-strip-smoking-and-hollering-obscenities antics to be liked, to get ahead in life, or, most of all, to be a happy, fulfilled person.

Now, perhaps Mandy and Heidi turned out to be really sweet, refined, well-rounded individuals. I haven't kept up with either of them, so I can't say for sure, but I'm guessing they're still manipulative and selfish and using their feminine wiles to get what they want (which would only add to my best friend's comical theory that anyone who was popular in junior high is doomed for failure in adulthood). Perhaps they eventually found their groove and individual passions, but there seemed to be a whole lot of unnecessary idiocy during those crucial years between puberty and college.

Actually, on second thought, I think I *can* almost guess

what kind of people Mandy and Heidi turned out to be: the kind of girls that make headline news every day on MTV—and I think we all know of whom I speak. Even if we don't pick up *People* in the grocery store line, we can catch the Stupid Girls' most recent fender benders, lawsuits, or jail time on the evening news. Sure, it's easy to laugh about a pop star's latest run-in with the law over lunch with our friends and read about the latest hook-ups in *Us Weekly* while we're at the beach, but when all is said and done and the next generation of young women grows up not knowing anything different, we are going to have a problem on our hands. Intelligent and refined girls are by far the exception these days—shouldn't it be the other way around?

Hopefully this book is more than just a humorous personal guidebook—with any luck, it will also serve as a call to action. Let's stop groveling and making idiots of ourselves around guys. Let's start walking and talking with style and poise. Let's stop letting a few infamously twiggy icons dictate our dress and diet. Let's make intelligence look attractive! Can we do it? Again, I say, YES! But first, you must know what you're up against in a Stupid Girl world. It's easy to slowly slide into stupidity with just a few small, bad choices, so we need to be on the lookout for them ahead of time. Otherwise, in the moment, it can be extremely tempting to give in to mojitos that are too strong, skirts that are too short, and men that are too stupid. Enter exhibit A.

Let's imagine a typical social scenario—you've just arrived at the local club. You've got a table, a chair, a drink, and an audience. This shouldn't be a socially fatal equation, but for many girls, it is. There are two ways this scene could develop—the good way and the not-so-good way.

In a good scenario, you would simply continue to sip your drink, order some mozzarella sticks, chat it up with your friends (and possibly the waiter), and thoroughly enjoy yourself. In a not-so-good scenario, you would be scaling the cocktail table, ripping your skirt, spilling that drink, and making a fool of yourself singing an off-key version of "American Pie." For many girls, the question of what to do in this situation is puzzling and proves to be their ruin, but it's really not that tricky; the minute you hoist that stiletto heel up onto the barstool upholstery, you have crossed into Stupid Girl territory. Whether it be getting jiggy with it during happy hour at the local bar or scaling the speaker system at an outdoor Kiss concert, decisions like this ultimately determine your reputation as a charming young lady or a cheap floozy.

Exhibit B. Here's a for-instance that many of us probably encounter almost daily: the guy-I-have-a-crush-on-just-stopped-and-talked-to-me scenario. You're at the gym, sweating profusely and tripping down off the elliptical machine on your way to the Pilates mats, when *he* walks in. You've already predetermined that if he came in today you would say something to him (but are now seriously reconsidering after spotting the amount of sweat pooling off your forehead and onto your iPod). What to do next? Well, there are two ways this could play out—the good way and the not-so-good way.

In a good scenario, you would simply continue on your way to the yoga section, flash him a big sweaty grin, and possibly offer up a "Hey" on the way there. If he's interested, he'll take it from there. In the not-so-good scenario, you would jump said crush and flood him with small talk, compliments, and subtle marriage proposals. There's simply no need to pounce all over the poor sap; coming on like a crazy, desperate lady will only scare the poor boy away. What you really want to do is lure him in with mystery and intrigue . . . which we will talk more about later. In a word, the good scenario just might end in victory, with an exchange of numbers and a date invitation, while the not-so-good scenario might end in utter disaster with him slowly backing away from your overpowering approach, not to mention foul gym smell.

Another one of the big hurdles we encounter in our current Stupid Girl world is the issue of dress. With so many see-through tunics and threadbare halter tops, our options for overexposure appear to be endless, and judging by most billboards and ad campaigns, heck, we really don't even need to wear any clothes at all! But in reality, conscientious and chary planning yields the greatest outfits. For example, let's envision a common shopping dilemma—what should we wear to Saturday's social outing? Enter exhibit C.

In a good scenario, you might carefully choose a lovely knee-length dress that will look stunning on you at the big Saturday night event *and* still leave something to the imagination. You will be smiling confidently, knowing that you have made a good choice. In a not-so-good scenario, you might purchase a dress that's missing the middle half to conveniently leave your midriff exposed, in addition to a skirt that provides your cheeks the opportunity to make an appearance at some point during the evening, as well. To sum up, the outfit would most likely cause you to look like a hooker. You might be smiling when you arrive, but you won't be for long, since you're about to get kicked out of the party for being underdressed!

These are just a few of the many grueling conditions we'll be up against in the fight against the Stupid Girls. It's like that old Persuaders song "Thin Line Between Love and Hate," except I think in this case it's a big, thick line between smart and stupid. But rest assured that each time we make the right choice, it will get easier and easier. Sometimes it might seem more convenient to just give in and act, talk, and walk like them, but we need to try to think long-term here (as if anyone really needs to remind us to do that—we've all had our wedding colors picked out since kindergarten).

When all is said and done and we've fought the good fight and run the good race, what would we rather have our headstone say? "Beloved Wife, Mother, and Friend," or something more along the lines of "A Lot of Poor Choices Here"? I think the decision is clear.

I have learned that Stupid Girls are going to be everywhere. If it's not Mandy and Heidi in seventh grade, it's Kaylie in high school. Then it's Samantha in college and Caroline at your first job. And the list goes on. We'll probably never be able to escape them or change them, but we can certainly step up our game and provide a glowing example of what an It Girl really should be—confident, chic, and clever. It can be tempting to fall into their trap of "like, I don't even know what to do tonight" lingo or hours of mind-numbing *Real World* marathons, but if we continue to surround ourselves with other stimulating people, ideas, and activities, we'll successfully navigate the muddy waters of stupid together.

Correct me if I'm wrong, but I think that you and I are a lot alike. Rather than stumbling along this trail of tube tops, hangovers, and jail time, we would like to find success, style, and love—the classy way. Even though it goes against almost every depraved and self-indulgent trend in our current culture, we are uninterested in contributing to the mucky wasteland of fake boobs and hair extensions and would instead like to, if at all possible, attempt to leave the world a slightly better place than when we found it. We're even a little old-fashioned at heart and think that if that's a problem, it might be a good one—a problem that other young ladies in our generation could use more of today! Well, I'm here to tell you that we're not alone.

The adorable and talented Hayden Pannetierre says, "I think that, now more than ever, young girls need a good role model. My mom always says, 'You are the books you read and the people you surround yourself with.'" Famed singer-songwriter Suzanne Vega has said, "I think people are sexy when they have a sense of humor, when they are smart, when they have some sense of style, when they are kind, when they express their own opinions, when they are creative, when they have character." And the gorgeous and witty Lauren Graham says, "Perspective is the most important thing to have in life." There are millions more of us out there, too, and it's time that we stand up and be counted. We've sat on the sidelines for too long while our trashy counterparts scooped up all the local and national headlines with their buffoon-like antics and shockworthy scandals.

I'm not sure exactly how or when we got to this point (a mere fifty-some years ago, Lucille Ball's TV network wouldn't even allow her to be shown pregnant on TV—it just wasn't done!), but it is indeed a different world than Audrey's bygone era of pretty dresses, classy speech, and charming behavior. Rather than having a humble, gracious attitude toward fame and beauty, most girls these days throw every last piece of dignity out the window at the first sign of stardom and apparently find sex tapes just about as productive as an acting audition. Instead of pursuing dreams and goals with hard work and integrity, many fellow females feel a sense of entitlement and privilege and wind up shopping, partying, and sleeping their lives away. And while girls can be sweet creatures, I have little to no tolerance for the "spoiled princess" act. If you aren't familiar with this recently adopted royalty persona, check out MTV's *My Super Sweet 16* and be prepared to gouge your eyes out. Nothing is more unattractive than a rude, bratty, self-absorbed girl flashing her goods around the neighborhood and barking orders to her spineless parents and minion friends. Yeek!

Famed producer Julie Leifermann has said, "Having known Audrey, I have less tolerance for the star thing . . . if Audrey Hepburn can live on the road for three months, and be more talented than 99.9 percent of anybody on this planet, and come in and be on time and know her material and be delightful and professional and give you gold on camera—when I come across the behavior now, I have a really hard time with it. Celebrities today need to go to the Audrey Hepburn School of How to Be a Star."

So, what is it that motivates girls to act like deranged monkeys in tutus? Did their mothers pull their pigtails a bit too tight when they were little? Did some boys reject their second-grade love notes? Did they catch a glimpse of

Madonna in her pointy-bra getup and go batty? Somehow, in the last five decades we went from Eva Marie Saint daintily shimmying up the side of Mount Rushmore in a pintucked dress in *North by Northwest* to every quasifamous reality star "accidentally" leaking a sex tape online. It's actually a tad frightening when you think about it—in a mere fifty years, our legacy as levelheaded, engaging creatures has become twisted and warped to the point that the female gender (and the idiotic two or three who represent it most loudly) is almost laughable.

Parenting tactics have undoubtedly come into question with the glamorization of said celebrities' own blood relations, including Lynne Spears's unpublished memoir, the bizarre rise of Dina Lohan's own star, and the dubious actions of dozens of mothers on *The Real Housewives of Orange County.* Peer pressure is undeniably more intense than ever, and the widely accepted popularity of underage boozing and drug use certainly can't help the situation. The list is endless, and to be honest, I'm not sure that anyone knows exactly where we went wrong, but I am convinced that all hope is not lost.

Through hard work and high standards, we can become class acts that outshine the cheap stars. We can turn in our tube tops and gum chomping for pinstripes and promotions. We can ditch the party hats and all-night benders for burgeoning careers and real friends. As we step up to the plate, become more informed, and begin to influence those around us for the better, we will begin to see headline news stories that sound more like the following:

WOMAN DISCOVERS CURE FOR CANCER

GIRLS DOMINATE THE BUSINESS WORLD

HOLLYWOOD RETURNS TO OLD-SCHOOL CHIC

FEMALES LEAD THE POLITICAL MACHINE

FASHION MAKES A CLASSY SHIFT

ANOTHER NOBEL PEACE PRIZE
AWARDED TO LEADING LADY

This current rubble of mindless glitter girls and senseless nitwits has become the norm, and it would be easy to simply fall in line and conform to the times. No one expects much more out of young women these days, and when one does distance herself from the masses and present a respectable feminine image, she shines brightly above the rest. It wouldn't take a lick of effort to follow suit with the Stupids, but it will take guts and smarts to go beyond the status quo. Why? Because very few attempt to do exceptional things anymore. Not many put in more work for less pay. Rarely is anyone willing to be considered foolish and unpopular for the sake of dignity and self-respect, and a very select few dare to rise above the good to get to the great. So when we do exceed what's expected of us, it's only natural that we will stand out in the crowd.

I'm convinced that our new classy standards can raise the cultural bar and turn more heads than the Stupids' exposed bra straps. I am positive that our hard work and long hours can put to shame the popular purse-dog-shopping-and-sweatsuit-wearing. And I know that our witty, well-informed words can speak louder than the Stupids' collective strain of "OMG!" We do live in a different world from Audrey's time of pearls, full skirts, and record players, but I don't doubt that we can put style, class, and grace back on the map again. We *can* be Hepburns . . . even in a Hilton world!

Chapter One

Keep Your Chin Up and Your Skirt Down

"You have a good many little gifts and virtues, but
there is no need of parading them, for conceit spoils
the finest genius . . . the great charm of all power is
modesty." —*Louisa May Alcott*

Self-respect is one of the greatest assets a girl can
possess, and yet it's one of the biggest things we're
lacking these days. Oh, the shame that's been doc-
umented by reality TV crews all over the world! And the
drunken party pics that have been posted on MySpace
pages all across the Web! Not to mention the countless
cleavage-baring, club-hopping tops that have been pur-
chased on clearance! But despite the constant news cover-
age, no one actually wants to see crotches flashed while
females climb out of limousines and boobs spilling out at
the Oscars. Somewhere along the way, we've lost the art and
mystery of self-respect. So how do we get it back? Believe it
or not, there are many ways to be an A-list hottie without
giving it all away. It starts with leaving something to the

imagination, asking yourself if this is what you want to be remembered for, navigating the muddy waters of "new peer pressure," and finding out what guys *really* want. (Surprise! It's not what you think.)

One of the fastest ways to gain (or lose) respect is with your image. Think about it: when Mariah Carey tries to squeeze everything into that double-zero miniskirt from seventh grade, words like *classy* and *admirable* don't usually spring to mind. But when Jessica Alba dons an elegant, floor-length golden number that successfully covers all controversial body parts at the Academy Awards, she positively commands attention. Before we even open our mouths to speak, our clothes will always do the talking for us, announcing loudly whether or not we respect ourselves. It's true that you never get a second chance to make a first impression, and many of our first impressions are crucial ones—interviewing for a big job, meeting future in-laws, making an important business contact, going on a blind date. The first impression should be memorable . . . but in a good way!

We rarely hear about someone being judged for covering up too much skin, but when an attention-seeking star steps out in a see-through, low-cut dress, we all get to read about it in the next day's headlines. Wardrobe successes and taboos are always points for conversation, and when things are too tight or too small, when boobs are loosed and crotches are exposed, rest assured that people are going to talk. And in this case, it's best to be on the receiving end of flattering remarks and glowing compliments rather than getting the short end of the apparel stick. When in doubt about an outfit, err on the side of caution. People would be hard-pressed to find something bad to say when you look modestly glamorous.

So what is *your* image saying about *you*? Take the Hepburn Guide to Self-Respect Quiz to find out!

1. It's girls' night out, and you're doing dinner and a movie. You:
   a. Change into some Seven jeans and a cute new tunic
   b. Slip on a denim mini and a halter top
   c. Pull on your stand-by scrubs and sweatshirt
2. While you're waiting in the lobby for your big interview, you:
   a. Read *Elle* and try to sit up straight
   b. Make a beeline for the bathroom to apply more lipstick
   c. Suddenly realize that you shouldn't have worn flip-flops
3. After a successful first date with rich, handsome, has-to-be-The-One, you:
   a. Settle for a good-night peck on the cheek and wait for him to call

b. Jump him before he has time to think twice

c. Figure he'll never call back, and down a pint of Ben & Jerry's

4. When asked to strip naked for the new MTV reality show, you:

a. Politely decline and wait for your next fifteen minutes of fame

b. Don't waste a minute shedding those layers

c. Say no because you're positive you would look horrific

5. The celebrity you admire the most is:

a. Reese Witherspoon

b. Pamela Anderson

c. Kirstie Alley

Now tally up the answers and check the Hilton–Hepburn spectrum below. Are you closer to being an Audrey or a Paris?

If you picked mostly A's: With just a few tweaks, you could be a certified Hepburn! For the most part, you think Paris and her cohorts are ridiculous, and you aspire to be anything *but* that. You always work what you've got but never flaunt it to the point of excess. You have a classy sense of style, and you exude confidence wherever you go. You're smart, successful, and know what you want. Guys respect you for respecting yourself, but occasionally they might mistake your confidence for arrogance. Just don't forget to let down your guard every once in a while and take some chances in style, life, and love.

If you picked mostly B's: It seems that your Hepburn certificate may be temporarily revoked, but that's okay. We can work with that. You might own a few tops cut down-to-there, and you seem to always find yourself in an endless circle of bars, boys, and broken bra straps. The world of Paris, Lindsay, et al. reminds you a lot of your own life, but you're not sure if that's a good thing. To start attracting the type of guys you'll want to date and the kind of girls you'll want to be real friends with, you need to start with developing some self-respect. With a little image tweaking and some old-fashioned words of wisdom, you'll soon have a newfound confidence and become an It Girl.

If you picked mostly C's: You could probably not care less about being a modern old-fashioned girl right now. You're smart, headstrong, and are not usually impressed with social requirements and trends. You're not concerned with Paris or her friends and don't really care what outfit fits best in the bust or if the shoes match the bag. You have a healthy measure of self-respect; it's just not being channeled into the image you project. But by the end of this book, you won't be able to contain your new poise, and you'll discover that Hepburn style can be surprisingly comfortable *and* chic.

Thanks to the fact that we're diverse, the smart, sophisticated girl-world is going to look a little different to each of us; we wouldn't want it any other way. Not one of us is going to look exactly like Audrey Hepburn, and that's just fine. We can pursue class, style, and grace in our own distinct ways. The legendary Judy Garland said it best: "Always be a first-rate version of yourself, instead of a second-rate version of somebody else." We're all starting out at different points on the classy, stylish, and graceful spectrum, but no matter where you're at, you can simply make small changes. Whether you're still shopping at Abercrombie or already completed debutante training, there's no such thing as too far gone.

The great thing about living with class, style, and grace is that it has nothing to do with wealth. Being classy is an attitude and outlook on life; the art of gracefulness is how we behave and act when no one is watching; being stylish is how we present ourselves to others. It might involve our clothes, but it's not defined by designer labels. It might include our job, but it doesn't matter if we are white-collar or blue-collar. It might entail a different set of social obligations, but it's not dictated by where we were raised. Why? *Because class is not defined by our circumstances—it's our reaction to those circumstances that defines who we are.* It doesn't matter if you work at McDonald's or the Trump Tower—are you punctual and courteous? It is not a matter of whether you went to an exclusive private institution or a free public school—did you make the most of every opportunity given to you? It doesn't make a bit of difference whether you're designing clothes for Vera Wang or working in the fabric section of Wal-Mart—are you attentive and accommodating? No matter what your upbringing was, what your current friend situation looks like, or what your yearly income is, you can do this. I don't care if you're living in a 550-square-foot apartment in Lincoln, Nebraska, or in a penthouse on Park Avenue. It doesn't matter if you're scraping by on minimum wage or raking in a six-figure income. You can live with style, class, and grace no matter where you are, who you know, or what you do.

One of the greatest benefits of living with confidence and self-worth is that we don't need to constantly rely on others for fulfillment. Many of our lady counterparts feel the need to tinker about in the teensiest tops known to man for attention, or be constantly snockered or high to have fun, but when you naturally feel good about yourself, you can focus on being the fabulous female you are, rather than seeking approval from every Tom, Dick, and Harry. Journalist, essayist, and novelist Joan Didion very accurately said, "To free us from the expectations of others, to give us back to ourselves—there lies the great, singular power of self-respect." It's a freeing mind-set to no longer have to derive our value from others.

So how do you start implementing a modern yet old-fashioned level of self-respect in your life? Author Stacey

Charter says, "Don't rely on someone else for your happiness and self-worth. Only you can be responsible for that." Clearly, if we didn't get it from our parents earlier, they probably aren't going to start doing it for us now. Our friends can provide support, but they can't be the instigators (although it would be a fun concept to try together!). And as much as we are trained to believe that guys will bring fulfillment to our lives, they won't bring everlasting happiness, either. We won't find it in short skirts or catcalls or lap dances or one-night stands—it has to start with us. If you don't respect yourself, no one else will.

One of the best ways to cultivate a healthy self-image is by celebrating your positive and unique qualities. Try a few of the following exercises to further confirm your lovely, distinct traits and characteristics.

- 👍 *Take a personality test.* I'm obsessed with taking personality tests—you can discover so many fun facts about yourself, new facets that you may not have seen before. Whether it's a Myers-Briggs or a "9 types" test (my personal favorite), take a minute to answer a few questions—you might be pleasantly surprised!

- 👍 *Ask a friend.* Get a close friend or family member to list some of your most admirable gifts and unique traits. I think they called these "warm fuzzies" in elementary school.

👍 *Identify other positives.* List the characteristics of someone you admire, whether it be a first lady or your grandma. Which of those characteristics do you see in yourself? What areas do you want to improve on?

👍 *Find your niche.* Identify something you have to offer the world that no one else can. At the risk of sounding like a hokey self-help guru, I am convinced that every person has a unique set of gifts specifically designed to contribute to the world, and if those gifts aren't used, a void will go unfilled.

👍 *Get out.* One of the best ways to instantly boost your mood and self-image is to get a little fresh air. Especially if you're experiencing the day-in-and-day-out buzz-kill of fluorescent office lighting, just half an hour of natural sunlight will do wonders for a sagging attitude.

👍 *Educate yourself.* To quote the old Saturday morning PSAs, "the more you know," the better you feel about yourself. Get informed on political issues, global needs, current events, and even new books and movies, and feel your confidence expand.

👍 *Give it away.* Do something nice for someone else. Surprise a pregnant coworker with a baby gift, help an elderly neighbor take out the trash, take your mom on a lunch date—nothing will boost your self-respect more quickly than a random act of kindness.

Now that we're committed to putting self-respect first, what's the next step? Like we determined before, our outward appearance makes the first and strongest impression, so let's go there.

First things first: we all need to have a debriefing on our wardrobes. I'm unsure of the exact origin of the phrase "leave something to the imagination," but I *am* sure that these are words of wisdom. I know it's enticing for us to show off our young, hot bods, but never underestimate the power of some cleverly concealed skin. Many of my well-endowed friends have said that they're continually tempted to prop up the girls on a virtual V-neck shelf, so we went in search of a more flattering fit and found it! Try on a scoop neck for size instead of your usual plunger (J.Crew has them in a myriad of colors). Or perhaps you're a compulsive short-skirter? Try branching out with a sleek and sophisticated pencil skirt (Banana Republic has yet to fail me in this department).

If you really insist on going up-to-there on your lower half, why not add a full-coverage, flowy blouse on top? (Hit up BCBG for one of these.) Or try a kitten heel (Target, baby!) once a week in place of your five-inch stilettos and your feet will thank you, too. And if you're going to exercise your right to bare arms (and cleavage) on top, opt for a wide-leg trouser pant or tailored pair of dark-rinse jeans on the bottom (Anthropologie's selection of wide-leg pants is unrivaled, in my opinion). Rather than putting it all out there, let's leave the people wanting more. When in doubt, don't let it all hang out!

Next, we ladies need to stand up straight. Good posture instantly inspires respect and gets attention. You won't believe what good posture will do for your image (think Nicole Kidman). So pull those shoulders back and hold your head up high. You'll feel like you've undergone an instant makeover, and you'll look like it, too—great posture can make you instantly appear five pounds slimmer! And not only will you *appear* more confident, you'll *feel* more confident.

To make things easier, when you leave the house each morning, make a mental note to walk taller (or leave yourself an actual note on the door). Then try replacing that stiff executive desk chair at the office or at home with a core-strengthening, posture-improving exercise ball (I recommend the FitBALL Plus in Pearl—it doesn't pick up dust bunnies!). Then sign up for a yoga or Pilates class with a girlfriend, and within a week you'll feel inches taller and be gliding along the sidewalks like Gwyneth Paltrow. Add a two-inch heel and you may well be truly unstoppable.

Lastly, work on making eye contact. It's just a tiny detail, but it could make the difference between being just another shifty-eyed shrinking violet and getting that big job! I work in the music industry and have conducted countless media-training sessions with artists and bands, and one of the first rules of thumb they are taught is to maintain eye contact with the interviewer or audience. I have personally seen the positive effects of eye contact (Faith Hill is great at it) and, likewise, the adverse effects of little to no eye contact. One particular artist (who will remain unnamed) actually looked down and texted his manager throughout the entire course of an interview with a major music publication. Not surprisingly, his next album did *not* receive a good review from that magazine!

Good eye contact personally connects you with your audience and cuts physical distance in half, so make it a point to lock eyeballs with friends when they're talking, with dates over dinner, and with your boss while he's giving you an assignment. Whether you're at an interview or a cocktail party, eye contact with fellow conversers will communicate intelligence and aplomb. Not only will you appear more personable, you'll have an instant air of confidence and self-possession. Confident girls who conduct themselves with style and grace are memorable, and when you make eye contact with those around you, you'll be hard to forget.

In the eternal words of Momma Aretha: R-E-S-P-E-C-T! Besides being a flat-out brilliant song (as well as the obvious anthem for any self-empowerment campaign or story), the message is still clear and relevant, forty-some years after its release date. Aretha did it, and now we're going to find out what it means to us!

Our current shopaholic/clubaholic/talkaholic culture is very different from our grandmothers' world of sock hops and petticoats. It can take years to build up trust and gain respect from others, and those gains can be lost entirely with just one bad move. Between all of the get-famous-quick reality shows and drunk-and-disorderly MySpace pics, it's easy to do some irreparable damage with just one lax step. For example, thanks to YouTube, Miss South Carolina will forever be known as that girl who flubbed the map question. Not to mention the endless stream of *The Bachelor* contestants that have made permanent champagne-'n'-hot-tub spectacles of themselves on national television. And, of course, Paris Hilton has yet to live down her infamous "night in Paris." These respectability slip-ups, however, do not have to happen to *us*. Respect and self-respect stem from discipline, and discipline is all about the little (and big) choices we make every day. And the big ones might not be as difficult to make as you think.

First of all, we need to always ask ourselves what we would do if our grandmothers were here. Would Grandma approve of that audition tape for *The Real World*? Doubtful. How about the miscreant boy you dragged home last night? Probably not. Or how about a Coyote-Ugly-tabletop birthday dance? Definitely a no. I've finally figured out that somebody is always watching, always judging our actions, and sometimes that someone turns out to be our boss, our little sister, or, yes, our grandmother. After years of building our reputations as hard workers, intelligent students, and the world's greatest daughters, why would we want to throw it all away for one impulsive low?

When it comes to understanding consequences, Anne Hathaway, teen princess turned red carpet staple, sets a great example: "I really don't drink, I don't do drugs. I feel like right now I've been given so many opportunities I don't want to mess it up with those things." I have concluded that no opportunity is so worthwhile, no circumstance so urgent, that it should make us ditch our values and convictions. It may be tempting to post those pictures on MySpace, but many employers now scan potential employees' profiles and make decisions based on what they see. It can be tons of fun to go out clubbing until the wee hours on a Wednesday, but does your job depend on you being on time in the morning? And as much as I love reality TV, I've realized that I don't really want to be remembered for an embarrassing, short-lived stint on VH1 or YouTube. Whatever you decide, just make sure that you set your standards high and stick by them no matter what.

Now, we're respectable dames, but that doesn't mean we can't have any fun. Call us what you will—do-gooders, prudes, goody-two-shoes (do people still use that term?)—

the quintessential good girls always get a bad rap for being dull, priggish, lame, and stuffy. But I've got a lot of friends who could give Tina Fey and Amy Poehler a run for their comedic money. Just because we aren't letting it all hang out on national television or getting sauced and making out with the copier repairman in the break room doesn't mean we can't have a good time! So in celebration of our tasteful craziness, I've listed a few (tried-and-tested!) classy, graceful, and stylish alternatives that will solidify your It Girl status yet leave you feeling regret-free the next day.

1. The next time the gang goes out for the night, try springing for a virgin Bellini during rounds two and three instead of the usual martini. It's one of my favorite non-alcoholic drinks (my husband used to be a bartender, so I've made him fix me every yummy nonalcoholic concoction in the book). This sweet, peachy/beachy drink is fun, tasty, and pretty to look at. But best of all, you'll remember how you got home! Try it during your next night out, and even if the girls are coming over for a fun night in, whip up the quick, easy recipe at home.

Virgin Bellini

1 part peach syrup
3 parts Sprite
Ice cubes

Dash of cherry grenadine
Maraschino cherries (optional)

1. Pour peach syrup and Sprite into blender with ice that is equivalent to the liquid level. Blend.

2. Pour into tall champagne flutes and add a dash of cherry grenadine for flavor and color.

3. Serve with maraschino cherries (optional). Bottoms up!

2. The next time *Rock of Love* comes on (I'm sorry, that has to be one of the worst reality shows of all time) and you start seriously contemplating lowering your IQ for a brief fifteen minutes of fame, flip over to something expletive-free and halfway stimulating, like a do-it-yourself home-makeover show on HGTV. Take a quiz at their online Web site to discover your own interior style, and register you and your roommate for a shot at the show and an interior-design makeover. They won't even make you take off your clothes!

3. If you're like me, when you're not working at your computer, you're probably on there IM-ing, or Facebooking, or online shopping. It's only natural to be occasionally tempted to upload last spring break's racy late-night pics to your Facebook profile. But rather than giving in

to idiocy when you get the urge, head on over to your e-mail account instead and type up a quick message to your best friend from high school that you haven't said boo to in ages. Chances are you have stuff to catch up on, and it will make her day to hear from you!

4. Have you recently been contacted by a sleazy K-Fed sort (who you would usually never give a second thought to, but you're lonely)? Don't let yourself give in to desperation! Otherwise, you'll soon end up like Michael Scott on *The Office:* "What's it like being single? I'm optimistic, because every day I get a little more desperate, and desperate situations yield the quickest results." Nooooo! There is absolutely no reason whatsoever for someone as classy and fabulous as you to stoop to desperate lows just because you're beginning to lose hope in the male gender. Rather than spending the night with some deadbeat, show him the door and go buy that great pair of boots you've been wanting (feel free to sing *R-E-S-P-E-C-T!* on the way to the store).

5. It can be disheartening when it appears as though every normal young lady now has the boobs and behind of a Greek goddess. Have you even been feeling tempted to enhance the girls, along with Heidi Montag and so many other females? When those of us who *have* stuck with what nature gave us start to feel like chopped liver,

certain options can begin to be appealing. But rather than blowing all your savings on a shoddy boob job, just pick up a few push-up bras from Victoria's Secret and spend the rest on a cruise to the Bahamas. You'll be tan, happy, and silicone-free!

If we think that we are the only ones who benefit from our classy choices, we're wrong. One of the rare tactful, graceful, and stylish girls in Hollywood today, Reese Witherspoon, has said, "Creating a cultural icon out of someone who goes, 'I'm stupid, isn't it cute?' makes me want to throw daggers. I want to say to them, 'My grandma did not fight for what she fought for just so you can start telling women it's fun to be stupid. Saying that to young women, little girls, my daughter? It's not okay.'" Self-respect isn't just for us, for the now. It's also for the preservation of the dignity, class, and fabulousness of femininity for future generations of young women.

My younger sister said to me a while back, "If we think female role models are bad now, can you just imagine what it's going to be like when *we* have kids?" Yeeek. Do we really want our little nieces to have no better example to look up to than pole dancers and Hooters calendar girls? Who will our own daughters beg for an autograph from? Some rogue Disney Channel actress who freely offers up naked cell phone pictures? To ensure that our nieces, our little sisters, and our future daughters don't grow up to be Girls Gone Wild, let's keep our self-respect levels high and give them something to look up to.

The next time we're confronted with a sticky situation, we need to ask ourselves—is this really what I want to be remembered for? Is this what I want my kids to remember me for? My parents? My grandchildren? Horace Greeley, an American newspaper editor in the 1850s, said, "Fame is a vapor, popularity an accident, and riches take wings. Only one thing endures and that is character." Let's muster all of our newfound self-respect and make our lives count for something more than silly shenanigans and late nights at the club.

If the personal benefits of self-respect aren't initiative enough to up the class factor, then the lure of a potential boyfriend always seems to do the trick! While it appears that, many times, guys can't see past the short skirt in front of them, most men (well, the ones who are worth your time) are more perceptive than we give them credit for. Would an average red-blooded male really pick a self-respecting girl over a slutty one? Survey says: Yes!

Most of us have been tricked into thinking that all men are simply in it for the legs, boobs, and sex, but you might be surprised to find that the majority of guys have more in mind than just patches of exposed skin. I just heard that, if given the choice between meeting the love of their life or having great sex for six months, almost every single guy would pick meeting the love of his life. John Mayer (I'm going to go ahead and say right now that *Room for Squares* pretty much got me through the eleventh grade) has said, "Every guy wants a girl and a relationship with . . . real trust." He later went on to say, "I'm looking for my ideal soul mate. That is somebody who is confident enough to feel love at a moment when love is not being given. A lot of times, I feel like I'm on the road to support a family I don't even have yet. I don't have to tour as much as I do, but I want to for that future family." We're not the only ones who dream about finding "the one" and settling down with 2.5 kids and a nice picket fence!

Though it may not seem like it at times, many other guys would also prefer a smart, self-respecting girl they could take home to their mom, as opposed to Rhinestone Barbie. One of my close guy friends even told me once that "most guys aren't actually interested in cheap girls." He went on to disclose that while they might be "fun for a while," they will probably never make it home to Mom, because guys ultimately want an interesting, self-respecting girl who can hold a halfway intelligent conversation.

Out of curiosity, I posed the question to several other guy friends and coworkers in a casual, informal environment (and was certifiably shocked by my findings!). I asked, "When given the choice, would you prefer a girl who is simply nice to look at from behind, or one you could take home to your mom?" To my pleasant surprise, *every one of them* said they would prefer the girl next door. It did satisfyingly shock me and slightly rejuvenate my belief in the male gender—the majority of guys really might prefer a smart, down-to-earth girl with a sense of humor to a busty airhead that will give it up on the first night. Bravo, boys! You guys really *can* tell the difference between a girl with self-esteem and smarts, and a pinup with a short skirt and an airbrushed manicure.

So if we want their undivided attention for about 2.4 seconds, we should keep wearing our glittery minis and doing the bend-and-snap. But if we want a real relationship with a real gentleman, we should just keep being our smart, classy, fabulous selves and they'll be beating down our doors in no time.

But what about those guys out there who are just in it for the mindless sex? Well, I don't know about you, but I personally wouldn't want to be with a guy who doesn't respect me, let alone care if I respect myself. These idiots are obviously not worth your time. For those who feel some kind of bizarre need to jump in the sack to prove just how much you love him anyway, a good note to keep in mind is that *if they don't want us without the sex, they're not going to want us with it.* Feel free to tape that to your bathroom mirror and read it every morning. If they're not really into you before hooking up, hopping into bed with them is not going to change anything. A jerk is a jerk is a jerk. It's time to stop being stupid and giving it up on the first date—it severely docks those classy, stylish Hepburn points!

If there's one thing that we intelligent, beautiful, and

funnier-than-heck girls are *not*, it is desperate. A Hepburn doesn't need a piece of arm candy to walk tall or a strapping boy to make her life complete. No woman should ever have to convince a guy to want to be with her—*ever*. If a guy isn't into you, who cares? It's his loss. Cut him loose and move on already. The lovely Jennifer Aniston has said, "A relationship isn't going to make me survive. It's the cherry on top." Sure, I've blubbered for a few days over a lost love, but that was from a breakup that I instigated; in no way do I advocate crying into bowls of Ben & Jerry's for weeks over a rejection that came from someone else—any guy who has driven you to that point isn't worth your precious time, emotions, or Kleenex!

Case in point: One of my old interns would often chat with me about her continuous cycle of boy woes, and after a particularly pathetic and painful conversation, I realized it was time to slap some common, self-respect sense into her. She spouted off the following discourse, proving once and for all that desperation is attractive on no one:

> So, try to make sense of this one, Jordan. I called this guy Jake to ask if he would like to go out to eat on Friday and he said that he was busy studying. So, I asked how long it would take him to study and he said it would probably take all night long. But I figured he would probably need a break and want some food later on. So I called him later, around nine p.m., and asked if he was done studying

yet. He said he was still really busy and couldn't go, but I decided just to drive to his house and surprise him anyway. So, I drove out to his house [author's note: said boy lives *thirty-five miles* away] and he said he still couldn't go! But I dragged him out of the house and drove him to a restaurant and can you believe what he said? He said, "You know, I like having you as a friend, but I just don't want to hang out this much." And I was like, "Well, we don't actually hang out that often, I've been trying to call you for a week and you're always busy." And he said, "Yeah, I'm just really busy right now and should get back to studying." Jordan, can you believe that? It's not like I'm asking him to marry me, I just like hanging out with him!

Ohhhh, where to start? Besides being obnoxious, she was practically waving the big red "I'm desperate" flag in this sweet boy's face. She was groveling and pleading—not a pretty picture. Her first clue to stop should have been that *she* had to call *him* (which we'll talk more about later). Next, his "Friday night studying" excuse should have immediately tipped her off. (Have you ever known a guy who chose to spend his Friday night studying rather than hang out with the love of his life? That's what I thought.) Then, his endless stream of "thanks, but no thanks" responses should have indicated that she'd crossed the line into desperate-weird-stalker territory. And finally, his "I just want to be friends" speech was the nail in this relationship's proverbial coffin.

After tactfully suggesting that she stop calling and beating down this poor boy's door, I hinted at how unattractive desperation is. This boy was obviously becoming smothered by her constant clinging and lack of self-awareness, and it's difficult for guys to want more when we won't give them a minute to breathe. (We'll talk more about that later, too!) I can see why lover boy chose to give her the cold shoulder. It is highly possible and strongly Jordan-recommended to keep that self-respect intact by not begging for affection. A Hepburn doesn't *need* that guy and shouldn't lower her standards by becoming embarrassingly desperate. And if you think that guys can't tell . . . well, apparently they can.

One of my good friends, Brett, was the object of every girl's desire in school. He was one of those dark-haired, blue-eyed, naturally tan specimens that attracted the kinds of girls who would line up to fall over themselves in front of him. I always found it a comical scene and was especially intrigued by the fact that he never showed the slightest interest in any of them. So one day over lunch in the cafeteria, I finally decided to broach the subject.

"Why don't you ever date one of these girls?" I inquired.

"What girls?" he asked cluelessly as he dug into his salad.

"Oh, I don't know . . . just the horde of girls that follows you around drooling and hanging on your every word," I said, more sarcastically than I'd intended.

"Ohhh, *those* girls. Well, I don't like any of them," he stated matter-of-factly and went back to shoveling in ranch-covered romaine.

"You don't like them? Why not? They're all obviously in love with *you!*"

"Well, Jordan, that's kind of the problem." He shrugged in a nonhelpful, matter-of-fact manner.

"Why is that a problem? Don't you want a girl that's interested in you?"

"Well, yeah, but they're beyond interested. I think they, like, really like me. And that's not fun for a guy. You want a girl that makes you work for it a little bit. Those girls just all seem desperate."

A-ha! A lightbulb went on in my head that morning during lunch with Brett. Boys *can* tell. So the next time you become tempted to one-up the next girl at the club with a show of cleavage or call that boy for the sixth time in one night, it's imperative that you put away your boobs and your phone. Is desperation *really* the message you want to put out there? Let's display some classy, old-fashioned self-respect and refrain from doing either!

So you've been doing everything a good modern old-fashioned girl should—holding your head high, exuding confidence and poise, dressing with class and style, not throwing yourself at that boy at the bar—and you have yet to meet Mr. Right. Starting to wonder if any exist? Well, I have dug up several for inspiration and would like to share them with you.

James Marsden, the dimply actor/husband/father of two, is always eager to talk about his down-to-earth home life with his wife and kids: "I am always in the mood for my wife. Always." And of course there's the quiet Canadian boy who can actually make a dirty, scrappy beard look hot, Ryan Gosling. Of his relationship with Rachel McAdams he has said, "I mean, God bless *The Notebook*. It introduced me to one of the great loves of my life. Rachel and my love story is a hell of a lot more romantic than that." Honestly, Ryan, could you be any more perfect?

The same goes for Lifehouse's hunky front man, Jason Wade. On whether or not it's weird being viewed as a teen sex symbol, the blond rocker has said, "I guess it would be if I viewed myself like that, but I really don't. My wife doesn't, either. So we live this normal life. We don't really get caught up in that stuff." Josh Kelley, the singer-songwriter husband of Katherine Heigl (another modern, old-fashioned girl herself) has also said, "Now that I'm older, I draw from things like getting married and relationships." Kelley says that he used to find inspiration in other musicians, but on his most recent album, the southern boy talks "about the process of becoming a real man, getting married and taking the plunge." Hooray for real men!

Lastly, my favorite example is my husband, Drew. Besides being wildly funny and devilishly handsome, he is the epitome of a real man who isn't afraid to step up to the plate. Even though I barely knew him (and had already rejected him twice because I was convinced he was too quiet and shy!), I received a real letter in the mail from him that said, "Hey, Jordan, I know we just met, but I would really like to get to know you better. I think you're the most fun and amazing girl I've ever met and I'd love to take you out to dinner or a movie sometime. I'm going to call you later to see if you'd be okay with that."

Well, that about did it for me. Maybe I've read a few too many Jane Austen novels, but any guy who writes old-fashioned letters scores big points in my book. So don't get discouraged by the entourage of males that just hooted and hollered at you on the way back from your lunch break, or that creepy guy reading *Penthouse* in the store; there are plenty of classy, honorable boys out there. Just keep being your fabulous self, and before you know it, you'll find him.

Having good old-fashioned self-respect is undoubtedly the biggest hurdle to cross, and once we've got it, it will also prove to be the key difference between being a Hepburn or a Hilton. Self-respect is exactly what it says: respect for yourself. No one else can muster it up for you, but the minute you begin to tap into it, others will immediately take note, as it is a rare attribute these days. When we do respect ourselves, it's only natural that our attitude, wardrobe, and outlook on life will begin to stand in stark contrast to the cheap, disreputable Hilton world we live in. People will want to know what's different about you, so be prepared to tell everyone else the secret.

Chapter Two

Words, Words, Words

"I think, with never-ending gratitude, that the young
women of today do not and can never know at what
price their right to free speech and to speak at all in
public has been earned." —*Lucy Stone*

Great women like Abigail Adams, Ella Fitzgerald, and Anne Sullivan, who contributed so much to society and made so many advances for our gender, would probably be rolling in their graves right now if they could watch an episode of *I Love New York*. The sheer number of *likes* and *whatevers* would be enough to push anyone over the edge, not to mention the vulgarity and idiocy that accompany the majority of the verbal exchanges. Lucy Stone was right—we don't truly know the price paid by those who went before us. If we did, perhaps we'd try a little harder to squeeze an intelligent quip or two into conversation every once in a while! Perhaps we'd attempt to educate ourselves more about the political issues facing our generation. Maybe we'd step outside our comfy social bubble and learn about a different language, country, or culture. We might even begin to speak up about and work for issues that matter to us. Our voices are incredibly powerful tools, and we need to make the most of them!

Whether or not we realize it, people are always listening and judging the words that come out of our mouths. Your boss could be just around the corner while you gab in the break room about your wild weekend. Your impressionable niece might pick up an ugly phrase or two while you're candidly talking on the phone to a friend. And that date on Saturday night might not be so charmed by excessive usage of the f-bomb. All of these people (and more!) are constantly making assumptions about our character based on our daily tête-à-têtes, our uncensored musings, and our friendly chitchat.

So, how do you begin to rein in your words and sound intelligent? Mandy Moore is on the right track, having once said, "I want to go to college to study journalism. I want to speak French fluently, to travel. My mom was a journalist and it's in my blood." However, she may be a rare exception. It's certainly not trendy to speak well these days, as evidenced by any good *America's Next Top Model* episode. The current Hollywood-rich-girl mentality comes with its own neatly packaged vocabulary lesson, and any girl worth her Manolo Blahniks knows how to talk the talk and walk the walk. Most of our peers aren't making it a priority to improve their speech. It's a toxic, vicious cycle of "ummm, yeahs" and "like, totallys," and one of the only ways to break it is to get out of our cushy verbal comfort zone.

Carrie Fisher once said, "I was street smart, but unfortunately the street was Rodeo Drive." That could not be truer of today's young female population. The "as if" outlook on life portrayed in *Clueless* by Alicia Silverstone was once just an entertaining teen comedy, but it sadly seems to be more the norm now. Sure, Cher and Dionne were an amusing big-screen duo, and Jessica Simpson's tuna-chicken bit was worth a laugh, but I think we would all agree that life imitating art may not be the best thing—not when the art in question is a cable show with female characters under the age of twenty-five. Similarly, if we find ourselves being sucked into *Laguna Beach* vernacular around our friends, it may be time to break away from the posse for a while and search for more intellectual higher ground. Warning: this will not be easy. They will try to lure us back in with promises of mani-pedis and gossip magazines. But stay the course! Soon you'll be speaking like a Yale scholar. And when you're tempted to slip back into your old ways, just remind yourself, "If I wouldn't say this in front of my grandmother, I probably shouldn't say it at all."

To kick off our wordfest, take a crack at some of the following Smart Girl activities to get yourself thinking (and talking!) outside the box.

- Do a crossword puzzle every day over your lunch break.
- Pick up a learn-a-word-a-day desk calendar.
- Check out a foreign-language instructional CD from your library and pop it in during your commute to work.
- Play word games either online or with friends. My personal favorites are Scattergories, Catch Phrase, and Scrabble.
- Tape yourself talking—note any unnecessary or, like, filler words that you should, like, maybe not use.
- Intersperse some stimulating nonfiction books in your usual *Glamour* magazine and chick-lit routine.
- Read the dictionary during *Lost* commercials. That may sound extreme, but I actually used to read the dictionary for fun when I was little. Yes, I am *that* dorky.

Polite, respectful speech is a whole other dilemma. Boys get cruder with every *American Pie* movie, and ladies seem to stoop to new verbal lows every day. Novelist George Eliot once said, "Blessed is the man who, having nothing to say, abstains from giving us wordy evidence of the fact." I've met many girls who have nothing constructive or edifying to say yet average more words per minute than anyone I know. Evidently only a rare few are raised to employ etiquette or give gracious compliments anymore; if they were, reality shows would all but dry up due to lack of drama and sheer ridiculousness.

Now, I live in the South, so I actually do still witness

some courteous actions and proper etiquette on a daily basis. Boys are still taught to open doors for women, pull out chairs, and say, "Yes, ma'am" and "No, sir" from day one. Young women are still taught how to properly host a dinner party (we'll touch on that later!), how to decorate for the holidays, and how to make a mean batch of biscuits. (Side note: one of my best friends actually has to wear skirts every time she goes to visit her grandmother in Alabama because Mrs. Mabel still thinks it is "com-puh-lee-tely imprah-puh for a young lady to wear-uh showt pants.") I'll admit it—one of my favorite magazines is *Southern Lady,* whose target reader is probably about twenty years older than me; I can't help it—I love it. But I've been on the New York City subway enough times to know that respectful speech, polite manners, and proper etiquette aren't the requirement everywhere!

While you don't necessarily have to start using "Yes, ma'am" and "No, sir" on a consistent basis, a couple of easy, gracious phrases to implement are "please" and "thank you." It sounds like a kindergarten rule, but surprisingly few people use these simple, rudimentary manners anymore. I was particularly appalled while recently handing out Halloween candy to young trick-or-treaters at my in-laws' house. One boy around the age of ten (who wasn't even wearing a costume, by the way—come on, all you have to do is cut two slits in a white sheet!) came to the door and greedily reached into my pumpkin basket and pulled out a full-size

Kit Kat bar, then proceeded to dash off without so much as a "Trick or treat," let alone "Thank you." Not two minutes later, he was back ringing the doorbell, and when I commented, "Weren't you just here?" he replied, "Yeah, but I want some more."

Right then, my mother-in-law came to the door and sweetly replied, "Sorry, we have lots of kids coming tonight and we need to save candy for them."

The little rat then proceeded to retort, "Well I don't even like what you gave me before. I hate Kit Kats. Can't I have something else?"

At this point, I was about to lose it, but I calmly replied, "We only have Kit Kats or Hershey bars."

I figured that would close the case, but the ungrateful ankle biter only continued: "Well, I don't like those Kit Kats. How about I trade you something from my bag for a Hershey bar?" I was this close to reaching in his bag and taking that Kit Kat right back, but I refrained. I settled for simply letting him root around and pull out a Hershey bar in exchange for the aforementioned Kit Kat. Besides being miffed at his blatant ungratefulness, I couldn't believe the audacity and rudeness coming from such a young person. Besides determining to revisit every good and proper manner I'd been neglecting lately, I also silently vowed to teach my own kids the importance of etiquette and manners when the time comes!

In the meantime, etiquette can start by simply reinstating a "please" the next time you ask a coworker to hand you the stapler. You can offer a sincere "Thank you" to the waiter who brings your food. Try being a gracious driver and letting the car ahead of you into the traffic-jam line. Compliment the grocery-store cashier on her manicured nails. Offer an elderly person or pregnant lady your seat in the waiting area. These are such rare occurrences and expressions these days that it just might make that person's week!

In terms of proper and not-so-proper speech and language, I'm afraid that other common southern phrases, such as "We're fixin' to leave" and "I got a hankerin' for some grits" might cancel out the properness of formalities like "Yes, ma'am" and "No, sir" here in the South. It seems that we folk below the Mason-Dixon Line are continually searching for middle-ground lingo somewhere between the formal sweetness of Scarlett O'Hara and the blatant grossness of Jeff Foxworthy. Many of my friends have even made it their goal to ditch the accent entirely, but you certainly don't need to go that far and completely lose that congenial southern charm. You can stay true to yourself and still polish up your speech. Same goes for Yankee girls!

My husband is from Minnesota (or as they say, Minnes-o-o-o-ta), and now, after having spent lots of time there (I pretty much make him drive alternating routes between the Mall of America and the nearest Caribou Coffee), I've come to find just as much amusement in their extreme-north vernacular as I do in southern speech: "Ya sure, you betcha," "O-o-h that mo-o-vie was super great," and "Yer gonna hafta see this!" Again, I would never want them to fully lose their Minnes-o-o-ta-ness. We can all make some painless improvements to our current patois to clean up the edges.

Honestly, when was the last time you heard someone talk and thought it was really beautiful? A mere twenty-some years ago, Margaret Thatcher eloquently stated, "We are coming slowly, painfully to an autumn of understanding. I hope it will be followed by a winter of common sense." But, of course, very few have ever heard those words—we only get bombarded with Paris Hilton's riveting statement from 2004, "That's hot." Margaret's words sound like pure poetry, while P—well, let's just leave it at that.

So how do you avoid the Stupid Girl persona and cultivate a vocabulary that extends, like, past your *Us Weekly*? We'll delve into more details later, but you can start by turning off the TV, picking up a book, making a Smart Girl list, and staying informed. You can also try deleting a few "I dunnos" and inserting a couple more "I would be honored tos" in your daily rhetoric, just for good measure!

While television is without a doubt one of the many marvels of technology, it is also one of the quickest ways to rot the brain—it's called the boob tube, for crying out loud! They say that knowledge is power, and I'm pretty sure that one of the first steps toward gaining knowledge is turning off the TV. Don't get me wrong, I could easily talk myself into a *Hills* marathon any day of the week and, in all honesty, watch nothing but reruns of *Gilmore Girls* and *Seinfeld* for the rest of my life and be perfectly happy. But sadly, having the ability to list all of Rory's boyfriends in chronological order and do a mean impression of Elaine Benes isn't going to get me very far in life.

The other day, I had an epiphany. My sister and I grew up without cable and thought we were really roughing it, since our only two entertainment options were usually the local PBS telethon or *60 Minutes*. We pined for luxuries like the Disney Channel and Nickelodeon, and we listened with sheer incredulity to tales of a magical airwave called Cartoon Network. Typically, one of our friends would finally take pity on us and invite us over to spend the night, and we'd hungrily consume hours upon hours of *Clarissa Explains It All* and *Are You Afraid of the Dark?* Recently, though, I was talking about childhood stories with one of my favorite new bands that I work with at the record label. The group consists of four brothers in their twenties, and they actually grew up with *no* TV. Not just "we-only-had-one-in-the-family-room" or "all-we-had-was-a-black-and-white-set-in-the-kitchen" no TV. *Nothing.*

Now, these four guys are some of the most hard-working,

competent (not to mention attractive) young people I've met in a long time. I asked them the reason for their familial musical ability, and the lead singer, David, said to me, "Well, actually we're just really thankful that our parents didn't have a TV. Instead of plopping down in front of the television after school, we were forced to get creative—play instruments, practice, learn techniques from other musicians. We would never be where we are today if we would have had a television to watch." Well! That certainly gave me a new perspective on my own upbringing (I don't exactly have a record deal to show for my cableless childhood creativity, though, just a bunch of papier-mâché books about my two cats, Justin and Fluffy). It also made me think about how I might one day similarly discipline my own children. If cutting out a little *Rugrats* and *SpongeBob* makes my kids turn out half as smart (or good-looking) as those boys, my kids aren't gonna be allowed to so much as darken the door of a Disney store!

If you haven't quite reached the antimedia stage, I completely understand. And to be honest, I'm not at the point where I've eliminated *all* TV—I indulge in a *Lost* episode with my husband every now and then and still pop in an old *Friends* DVD every time I'm good and depressed. But it's easier than you might think to set small TV goals for yourself. If you're a daily consumer, try paring down your viewing to just a half an hour each day. If you watch only two or three shows a week, try just one. You'll be amazed at how many other things you have time for! But what do we do with all that free time? The possibilities are endless, but it can be tricky getting started.

When I first tried cutting out TV, I remember plunking down on the couch and staring vacantly at the blank screen, waiting for instructions as to what I should do next. It took me several weeks to get into a groove of doing *other* things first, rather than zapping on the tube pronto when I walked in the door. The easiest thing I found, and my first recommendation, is to *read a book.*

Several first ladies have advocated for book reading. The timeless Jacqueline Kennedy Onassis said, "There are many little ways to enlarge your child's world. Love of books is the best of all." Laura Bush is also passionate about promoting reading, saying, "A love of books, of holding a book, turning its pages, looking at its pictures, and living its fascinating stories goes hand-in-hand with a love of learning. Every child in America should have access to a well-stocked school library." But let's be honest: for some people, reading can be a daunting task. My mother was a reading teacher for thirty-three years, and before I could walk, I would crawl to our book drawer to read, so I'm probably a little biased, but I do know that the most common questions from my nonreader friends are about where to start. The huge sea of material to choose from can be overwhelming. To help you cultivate your inner bookworm, take the following quiz to find out which kind of book is best for you! Simply choose whichever answer sounds most like you.

1. If I have a free Saturday all to myself, I will usually:
   a. Ride my bike to the park or call up a few friends to go hiking
   b. Lay out at the nearest pool, beach, or open patch of grass
   c. Take a tour of the current art exhibit on display at the museum
2. When I'm surfing the Internet, I typically spend most of my time:
   a. Looking up airfare prices for my next spontaneous get-away
   b. Updating my Match.com profile and shopping online at Bluefly
   c. Reading up on the day's headline news while Googling that cute guy from the gym
3. When my roommate/significant other is gone for the weekend, my guilty-pleasure rental of choice is:
   a. *Blue Crush*
   b. *Legally Blonde*
   c. *Gone with the Wind*
4. If I could have dinner with anyone in the world, I would most likely pick:

    a. Lance Armstrong

    b. Penn Badgley

    c. The U.S. president

5. When I set foot in the mall, I make a beeline for:

    a. Foot Locker—my running shoes are currently being held together with duct tape

    b. J.Crew—hello, can anyone say "madras plaid"?!

    c. Sam Goody—the new Raconteurs album is out, and I can't read the liner notes on iTunes

6. If I won a free vacation anywhere in the world, I would:

    a. Take a safari in Africa—sleep under the stars, see wild animals, hike Kilimanjaro, etc.

    b. Relax in the land Down Under—soak up the sun every day, go snorkeling off the Great Barrier Reef, visit the Sydney Opera House, etc.

    c. Take an Old World tour of Europe—see the architecture, learn history, eat cheese every day, etc.

7. When I think of my dream house, I envision a:

    a. Rustic mountain home somewhere in the woods

    b. Beachy cottage close to the water

    c. Historic mansion that's been restored

If you picked mostly A's: Go get a suspense/thriller novel! You have a heart for adventure and are constantly on the go. You like being spontaneous and are quick, smart, driven, and perceptive. You love movies like *Ocean's Eleven* and *Signs*. A good mystery or suspense story with a well-developed plot will hold your attention, and you might enjoy authors such as G. K. Chesterton, John Grisham, Frank Peretti, or Tom Clancy. If you want a bigger challenge, pick up *The Lord of the Rings* by J. R. R. Tolkien.

If you picked mostly B's: You are a prime chick-lit candidate! You are easy-going yet passionate and probably enjoy shopping, laying out, reading magazines, and going for walks. You love to have fun and enjoy movies like *Bridget Jones's Diary* and *Sleepless in Seattle*. Lighthearted, humorous, and character-driven stories will keep you reading, and you'll really appreciate authors such as Jennifer Weiner, Sophie Kinsella, Anne Lamott, or Lauren Weisberger. For a challenge, try *Pride and Prejudice* by Jane Austen.

If you picked mostly C's: We've got a historic-fiction reader on our hands! You are a romantic and love reading about history, culture, and issues. You love to escape to different worlds and days of old yet appreciate a good sense of humor. You love movies like *Elizabeth* and *Sense and Sensibility*. Intelligent, well-written, and captivating historical fiction will keep you entertained for hours, and you may like authors such as Khaled Hosseini, Philippa Gregory, or Robert Hicks. If you're looking for a challenge, try *Gone with the Wind* by Margaret Mitchell.

If you're still not feeling the book thing, another great way to up the language ante is to learn a new one. Audrey

Hepburn knew several languages, including Dutch, English, French, Italian, and Spanish. However, if you're anything like me, your "foreign language courses" in high school roughly translated into three years of piñata parties and worthless workbooks. Just as we'd dive into *"Hasta mañana,"* one of the oh-so-mature boys would put on the classroom sombrero, run around, and taunt our teacher (who never could quite master the art of discipline) until she sent him to the office. All in all, I think I gleaned more about Spanish language and culture by watching Adam Sandler in *Spanglish* than I did in my three sad years of classroom learning on the subject.

So when I got around to really learning a new language, I decided to try one I was genuinely interested in. (I chose *Español* in high school only because other kids said that the German teacher would blow her cigarette breath in your face if you answered a question incorrectly.) I'd always been intrigued by the nation of Israel and thought that it might be exciting to try Hebrew, and I honestly had more fun in one week reading *Brandeis Modern Hebrew* than I did in all three years of Chips and Salsa 101. I've since fallen in love with the language and can't wait to visit Israel someday.

One of my best friends, Blair, spent nine months in Kyrgyzstan and upon returning to the United States enrolled in all kinds of Russian literature and language classes. She fell in love with their culture and wanted to experience as much of it as she could. Another good friend and coworker, Ruthanne, lived in China for a year, taught English in an elementary school, and still loves to talk about the culture, people, and languages, years later. Somehow, when it's a place or subject that is truly personal and fascinating to us, it's not work learning it. Even if you don't have the time or resources to take a year off and explore a foreign country, you can check out a language-on-tape program, read some travel memoirs, or subscribe to a monthly travel magazine from your country of choice.

Maybe your passion *is* a continuation of your French, Spanish, or German class in high school. Or perhaps you've always wanted to speak Italian. Do you have an interest in Japanese or Russian? Heck, why not try Mandarin Chinese? Or Dutch! The sky is the limit. You just need to find a language, country, or culture that genuinely appeals to you and immerse yourself in some great learning material from that society. Bonus: it gives you a really good excuse to take a vacation to that country once you're well-versed.

Journaling is another effortless outlet to improve your speech. Overall, people tend to filter out the "likes" and "umm maybes" when they're unconsciously jotting down their thoughts and feelings in a diary. Your natural self tends to come out more readily when you're alone with your thoughts and not influenced by outside speech, friends' conversations, music, and movies. I began keeping a daily journal in fifth grade, and it's one of the best things I've ever done. Not only is it superbly entertaining to go back and read about the things that were soooooo important to me at the time (I *for sure* wasn't going to marry Darin Chapman after he smashed a s'more in my hair on that field trip to the science museum), but you can take stock of how much you've grown and matured, even over the course of one year.

The journaling process can be extremely therapeutic. I think it's similar to the whole writing-an-angry-letter-but-never-mailing-it trick. A journal is a safe place to take out all our aggressions; my notebook has yet to complain about all the abuse I've heaped on it over the years. Journaling also provides some much-needed alone time for us ladies on the go. Most of us probably don't even get a lunch break to ourselves, so just a few precious minutes alone in the morning or before we hit the hay can truly have a cathartic effect. So go pick up a journal and keep it beside your bed. Make it a point to write a little something every day.

Besides documenting our hopes, our dreams, and our choice words about our boss, a journal also provides a perfect space to create a Smart Girl list! We talked about several small steps toward becoming a more intelligent, well-spoken lady, but now it's time to put them into action. Another of my coworkers and I sat down and did this about a year ago, and it's such a great, concrete way to articulate your goals. Just as an example, I've included my own list of things I'd

like to do to become a more articulate, knowledgeable, and
well-rounded person:

Jordan's Smart Girl List

1. Earn my master's degree
2. Learn how to live off the grid
3. Teach a college course on music and writing
4. Become fluent in Hebrew
5. Learn a new word every day

Now it's your turn. What's something you're constantly
thinking and wishing about accomplishing? Go buy an LSAT
study book and finally sign yourself up for the test! Volun-
teer to mentor a child after school! Read at least one book
a month! Take a French class and reward yourself with that
trip to Paris already! Take some time to really think about
your options and aspirations, and then grab a piece of paper
and ink out all your well-spoken, well-informed Smart Girl
goals. Then go do them!

Perhaps one of the most crucial aspects of learning to speak
with authority and intelligence is being informed. We've
all seen the sadly hilarious display of ignorance in Leno's
"Jaywalking" segments. In one episode, when asked, "What

famous character robbed from the rich and gave to the poor?" a girl responded, "Al Pacino." Another time, a young lady was asked the Pope's name and she responded, "Benedict Arnold?" Oooh, so close. And during a different segment, when asked the name of the ship that the Pilgrims sailed to America on, one girl replied, "U-Haul." When we're unaware of history and current issues, it's difficult to be knowledgeable on any subject. Becoming aware of the concerns facing our generation and understanding world events means flipping on the news instead of *Sex and the City*, picking up a book instead of a gossip rag, or maybe just engaging in a halfway stimulating conversation at work. Becoming an informed member of society means taking thirty minutes to cast a ballot in each election. It means getting engaged with the needs of our city, county, nation, and world. It means discovering our own opinions, passions, and voice and using them to impact events around us.

Ours has unfortunately become a generation of sheep. Rather than thinking for ourselves and working to unearth the truth in every situation, many of us blindly absorb the thoughts and stories dictated by the media. Rather than going along with our favorite celebrity's political endorsement, we need to do research and determine our own convictions on the issues. Instead of accepting mass-media reports as fact, we need to be willing to dig for the real information in each story. As opposed to simply engaging in the typical vernacular of the day, we can choose to take the high road and educate ourselves. My seventh-grade civics teacher had a poster that said:

> What's Popular Is Not Always Right, and What's Right Is
> Not Always Popular

I always loved that; it's so true. We can't assume that the current trend is always the best thing. Need proof? *Playboy* magazine. Unfiltered cigarettes. Crocs shoes, for Pete's sake! (Sorry, Mom, they look like a drain attached to a club foot.) Cultural values and rights are no different. Rather than taking them for granted, we need to become more informed and use our voices wisely.

Over two hundred years ago, novelist Ann Radcliffe said, "A well-informed mind is the best security against the contagion of folly and of vice. The vacant mind is ever on the watch for relief, and ready to plunge into error." That observation is more appropriate today than ever. Jessica Weiner, a brilliant author who writes beyond-hilarious material, also encourages women to take an active role in society: "We do have more opportunity open to us as girls and women, and yet we starve out this freedom, nip and tuck it, focus on the surface and don't show up to vote, protest, or make noise." True, it would probably be easier to simply float through life, blindly following the popular vote and remaining blissfully unaware of problems, issues, and impending evil, but that is what we like to call ignorance.

How do you achieve and maintain an informed mind? To keep from merely falling in line with society's group sentiments, it's important to educate yourself daily: sign up for an unbiased political blog, TiVo the evening news, set your laptop's homepage to a daily headline source, or go old-school and subscribe to a newspaper! We can become involved in our local government, vote regularly, contribute to a think tank, or simply donate time and energy to a cause that means something to us. Great women of history didn't put their lives on the line just so we could dance on tables and text boys all night long, so let's do them proud and start standing up, speaking out, and using our voices for good.

They say actions speak louder than words. That may be true, but one bad verbal slip-up could mean the end of a hard-earned reputation. Just look at poor Miss South Carolina and her infamous map flub! Let's begin upping the ante with our vocabulary, developing intelligent speaking habits and educating ourselves on issues that matter to us. Let's toss out those "likes" and "OMGs" and replace them with wittiness and aptitude. Let's speak lovely, ingenious words that make others sit up and take notice. Let's flip off the tube and crack open a book!

If you think that what we say doesn't matter, check out the following quote from an unknown source:

Watch your thoughts, for they become words.
Watch your words, for they become actions.
Watch your actions, for they become habits.
Watch your habits, for they become character.
Watch your character, for it becomes your destiny.

This is always a great reminder to me that our seemingly insignificant thoughts and ostensibly meaningless words have a profound impact on our future. Like Florence Scovel Shinn said, "Your word is your wand!"

After all of the reading, journaling, and self-informing you're doing, you will soon be speaking with smarts and bowling over colleagues, friends, and family members with your eloquent rhetoric and big vocabulary words. People will instantly take notice of your enlightened discourse, since it will be in sharp contrast to the majority of other young women's vernacular, and others will inevitably be attracted to, and want to join in, the pursuit of highly developed language. Despite the current slew of swearing, subpar oratory, and all-around Stupid Girl lingo, we *can* speak with class, style, and grace.

Chapter Three

Use Some Elbow Grease

"Nobody ever drowned in
his own sweat." —*Ann Landers*

While the current trend suggests that girls should simply laze about in pink sweatpants, eat bon-bons, and shop for ugly dog sweaters, I beg to differ. If success isn't built on long hours, big dreams, and good old-fashioned elbow grease, I seriously question its authenticity. Actress Sarah Brown made a brilliant statement that I absolutely love: "The only thing that ever sat its way to success was a hen." So funny and so true. But thanks to Hollywood's endless exploitation of real-life Malibu Barbies, it's easy to become disillusioned about hard work, good ethics, and real success. Can women still run offices, countries, and corporations? You'd never know it from watching MTV, but yes, they can.

It does seem that the only kind of success we hear about anymore is the my-parent-is-a-celebrity kind or the

I-went-on-a-reality-show type. A rare exception is Ivanka Trump, who, besides being perfectly gorgeous, has objected to comparisons to other certain hotel heiresses' infamous work habits: "I work 13-hour days for my money . . . I have a mortgage, you know. I think we are totally different individuals . . . If I were to go off the rails and become this party kid, I would not be able to afford my lifestyle. I've never had a sense of entitlement. I saw how hard my father worked for his money and it was always made very clear to me that things wouldn't just be given to me."

Unfortunately, that hard-work-doesn't-hurt mentality appears to be in short supply these days. Why? It's become painfully clear that our society just doesn't support a sincere work ethic anymore. At least in the entertainment industry, it really can seem to be all about *who* you know, not how *much* you know. Offhand, I can think of about five artists who have no business whatsoever singing aloud in public, let alone putting out an album, but because they know the right people, they've had a record deal handed to them on a silver platter. And it's painfully clear that you can bypass years of toil (and apparently common sense) just by being an heiress or the offspring of a rock legend, and Lord knows that you don't need a lick of formal training or education to be a staple in *People* magazine.

Like I said, I can't speak for other industries, but I would imagine that the business, education, financial, fashion, political, and journalism worlds have the same issue. That can be a tough pill to swallow, but there are definitely ways to be successful within that system. Does it appear ominous at first when we're barely perched on the first rung of the corporate ladder? Like a thunderhead filled with shrapnel! But that doesn't mean we should give up. In fact, it can make us more determined than ever to prove that hard work really does pay off in the long run. And there's probably only one place to start. You guessed it—at the bottom.

If you're anything like me, you probably didn't have the luxury of being raised by movie stars or high-ranking officials. Money certainly never fell from any trees in our backyard, and I can honestly say that I didn't have *one* name to drop when I set out to make my mark on the world. Not one. However, that can make our achievements that much sweeter. Likewise, Carley Roney, editor in chief of *The Knot*, didn't let her small-town upbringing stop her from pursuing success in the business world. "That was always my sensitivity: I don't have enough friends, I don't have parents with rich, well-connected friends, I didn't grow up in New York City, I'm some little country bumpkin here trying to make it," she says. "[My husband and I] had to do it by sheer hard work. We had to make it happen for ourselves." She has since gone on to create one of the biggest brands in marketing history, one that extends into TV, magazines, and online resources. Not too bad for a self-proclaimed country bumpkin.

My friend and corporate publicist for Warner Music Group,

Amanda Collins, attributes her success in a male-dominated business to having been surrounded by strong, confident, intelligent women her entire life. "Beginning with my mom, who rose to be the COO of the company at which she worked, and throughout my career, I have been encouraged by successful women who taught me that hard work and believing that I have the ability to effect change will allow me to realize my goals." Already established in a prominent position within the world's third-largest record label, she also says, "Business is business. What should matter is a person's ability to take business to the next level. When I walk into a meeting, I want people to see me for what I can contribute to the success of the company. I hold myself to that same standard and see my colleagues not based on their gender or background, but rather on their decisions, actions, and contributions to the team."

So how do we get from point A to *that*? One of the easiest ways to kick-start a career is by doing a little networking. Do you want to work at a magazine? Find out when the publisher's next social gathering is and make yourself available to chat with anyone and everyone there. Do you want to break into the music industry? Hit up a local songwriters' night in your area and make pals with fellow musicians and prospective label execs. Are you hoping to get that political-campaign gig? Join your candidate of choice's street team and start making an impact in your immediate community. Wherever your interest lies, don't be afraid to start small!

Another really great resource that isn't tapped into much anymore is mentoring. A mentor can be anyone, from an older colleague, to a pastor, to a relative—just someone you trust to give wise counsel and guidance. Mentors can be a *huge* source of knowledge and inspiration in the career-finding, soul-searching, mind-numbing period of complete befuddlement in our lives. So if you happen to find wise, caring, and trustworthy sources within your prospective industry, you should definitely draw on them for helpful hints, contacts, and all-around encouragement! You might be surprised to find that most people are more than willing to give recommendations, introduce you to prospective employers, and just generally be of service. It was a sweet, unassuming professor in college that not only encouraged me in my writing, but helped me land my first job in the music industry; I am still so grateful for him to this day.

My sister and I love this line that Kathryn Hahn delivers in *Win a Date with Tad Hamilton:* "It's like when I thought that I would never get that bartending job. My dad told me, 'Honey, your odds go up when you put in an application.'" Regardless of whether or not bartending is your final goal, the principle of the message remains: there is no substitute for simply *trying.* We can sit around and talk about all that we're going to accomplish, but unless we actually get out and do it, it won't happen. So when all else fails, put in an application!

When no amount of tips or advice succeeds in cheering

us, there's nothing quite like good old celebrity success stories to rouse our spirits. Just to show you that we're not the only ones who have had to pour our blood, sweat, and life savings into achieving our dreams, check out this word match. Try to pair up the correct success story with said person's former occupation. You might be surprised at what you find!

Tina Fey	Dunkin' Donuts employee
Courtney Cox-Arquette	Cold Stone Creamery server
Hillary Clinton	Model
Madonna	YMCA clerk
Julia Roberts	Piano teacher
Condoleezza Rice	Swimming pool store salesperson
Carrie Underwood	Babysitter
Lucy Liu	Canning factory employee in Alaska
Anne Hathaway	Gas station cashier
Martha Stewart	Aerobics instructor

Answers: *Tina Fey, YMCA clerk; Courtney Cox-Arquette, swimming pool store salesperson; Hillary Clinton, canning factory employee in Alaska; Madonna, Dunkin' Donuts employee; Julia Roberts, Cold Stone Creamery server; Condoleezza Rice, piano teacher; Carrie Underwood, gas station cashier; Lucy Liu, aerobics instructor; Anne Hathaway, babysitter; Martha Stewart, model.*

In my opinion, the most priceless image of all those is the Material Girl herself working the night shift at Dunkin' Donuts—oh, to have seen the top-selling female artist of the twentieth century surrounded by greasy cake pastries and sporting a DD visor. Priceless. Just goes to show you that everyone has to start somewhere (and now I want a donut). Anyway, those examples are a great testament to those ladies' hard work—clearly, they weren't afraid to get down and dirty to make a living, and we shouldn't be, either. In fact, the dirtier the better!

That old saying "A little dirt never hurt" extends beyond the days of getting sand thrown in our mouths on the playground. If you really want to succeed and pursue your passion, there's going to be a lot of long hours, sacrifices, and crying. You're going to have to cancel a few dates with the boyfriend, neglect a concert or two with the gang, and probably eat a few meals out of the vending machine. It won't be pretty for a while, my friends, but we'll get through it together. I never realized just what a problem it is for some people, though, until I met an intern I will refer to as Alana.

A while back, I was in desperate need of some help at work, and when I got a request from someone looking for an internship, I gladly hired the young lady. However, Alana (again, names have been changed to protect the ignorant) had a very tough time with this whole work-hard concept (and consequently, a very tough time finding a job later).

Besides consistently showing up late and putting forth little to no effort in her assigned tasks, she would often conveniently "forget" her purse. So she was driving everywhere without her license, and I was regularly forced to pay for her meals, CDs, and even parking passes! All I needed was a semi-intelligent gopher to run some errands and show up on time, but somehow I found myself reverting to my days of babysitting and telling her in a voice normally reserved for two-year-olds, "Okay Alana, we're going to leave for lunch at twelve today. Do you have your money with you? Are you all set to go?" One day, she even e-mailed and said she couldn't make it in to work that day because she watched a movie the night before, left her phone on silent, and consequently missed her alarm.

Needless to say, Alana did *not* receive a glowing letter of recommendation from me. In fact, she even inspired a top-ten list of ways to get fired! So before you reach for that snooze button on Monday morning, read on.

Top Ten Ways to Get Fired

10. Flash some kind of female anatomy part—any region will do.
9. Park in the CEO's reserved spot—they love that.
8. Smoke on the job.
7. Download *Titanic* to the network server.

6. Ask to be excused for the 2:30 showing of any movie.

5. Hit up IKEA on the company dime.

4. Mix cocktails at your desk.

3. Leave early on days that end in y.

2. Make everyone donate a dollar to "charity," then blow it all on your vacation.

1. Just don't show up at all.

Likewise, there are equally as many ways to go about making a good impression at work and keeping your job. First of all, be willing to go above and beyond the call of duty. There is a huge difference each year between my interns who do exactly what they're told and those that go out of their way to do more than I've asked. The former typically move on after the internship has ended with, at most, a polite letter of recommendation. The latter, many times, will receive a job offer. Those that do more than others expect or need always stand head and shoulders above the ones who do just enough to scrape by.

Second, don't be afraid to get your hands dirty with menial tasks. My old boss was the best at this. Even though he was the vice president of the department, he would join in on the unpleasant task of stuffing, addressing, and mailing out hundreds of CDs by hand every month. His encouraging, down-to-earth attitude was contagious and made the whole process a fun experience. You may very well be above licking those invitation envelopes for your boss's Christmas party, but make it a point to make them the best-licked invitations your boss has ever seen and soon you'll be moving on to bigger and better things.

Last, but certainly not least, keep a positive attitude. No one enjoys working with someone who constantly whines and complains, so unless you're being asked to clean your employer's dog poop out of the carpet (heck, even if you are!), try to keep a pleasant attitude. A smile and an optimistic outlook go a long, long way—you have no idea how much someone else at work might need to hear an encouraging word or just see a cheerful face.

In all fairness to Alana the intern, I've lived in both camps: whether you're knee-deep in the corporate rat race, simply starting out in the world of freelance work, or just trying to land that first gig, one of the most disruptive life changes when making the leap into the working world is arguably the schedule. When I first started my eight-to-five job, the six a.m. wake-up time was extremely disconcerting. The last time I had seen six in the morning was in high school for that choir trip when we all piled onto the bus in our bunny slippers to make our nine a.m. flight to New York. The whole process really does end up feeling a lot like Andy Sachs in *The Devil Wears Prada*; just when we drift off from the night before, we hear the loathsome alarm and groggily reach for the snooze button . . . morning after morning, consistently

seeing times of day that we never thought humanly possible and being so tired that we honestly can no longer tell
if we're asleep, awake, or just dreaming about being asleep.
The relentless routine of rising early and not-getting-home-
until-dark-thirty is a huge adjustment, not to mention the
fact that your life is pretty much over for five out of seven
days of the week. It takes specific rearranging of priorities,
commitments, and grocery shopping!

Aside from the weekends, those days of after-hours
club-hopping shenanigans are also definitely going to dwin-
dle (I'm kind of an eighty-five-year-old grandma at heart,
so late nights weren't too difficult for me to give up). And
since sleeping in is no longer an option, it takes only about
a week of two a.m. Waffle House runs and six a.m. wake-up
calls before you'll throw in the towel and succumb to the ten
p.m. corporate-world bedtime. But after you get the hang
of it, mornings aren't so bad. The sun is shining, the birds
are singing . . . all right, I'll be honest, now I'm one of those
obnoxious morning people who comes into work singing
"Zip-A-Dee-Doo-Dah" and talking about how great it is to be
alive. But the late-night sacrifices really are completely worth
it to know at the end of the day that we put our hearts and
souls into our work. And that is something that today's celeb-
utantes will probably never know. Alana might not, either.

Another notable lady has some wise words about hard
work and its rewards—my mother! While sending us out to

pick weeds or paint the garage, she would always say, "Hard work builds character! You'll thank me later for all the character you're building!" (And we begrudgingly have.) Paris and Nicole's *Simple Life*–fueled "hard work" arguably happened a little too late in life and probably didn't have the same effect. But for the rest of us, it really is a great principle to live by.

A new pop/hip-hop act I work with is a great example of how a little hard work really goes a long way. This trio of some of the most beautiful, eclectic, and talented people I've ever met has the most incredible stories of hard work and determination to make it. Blanca, the lead singer, was raised primarily by her mother after her father, a member of the notorious Latin Kings, left home when Blanca was young, and she was further mistreated by almost every male in her life. Manwell, the group emcee, grew up on the streets and soon got involved in robbing and stealing. Pablo had a near-death experience in a car accident and was surrounded by bad friends and bad influences. But all three of them chose to leave their old lives behind, blaze their own trail, and work twice as hard to get where they are today. They have since made it their goal to tell young people that anything is possible if you work at it, and it's no surprise that the phrase "I Have a Dream" has become their group motto and they even penned a song by the same name.

Venus and Serena Williams are another great example of the power of determination and hard work. After growing up in a rough LA neighborhood and practicing tennis on the neighborhood courts, the dynamic sisters have gone on to become two of the most successful and dynamic athletes in history. The girls' father used to tell everyone that one day his girls would take the tennis world by storm, and they did. But success didn't come before trouncing some vast odds and obstacles first. The girls' childhood neighborhood, Compton, is one of the most dangerous suburban areas in the United States; their sister was even killed by a gang member in South LA. But despite the overwhelming odds, they worked daily from the time they were little to make their goals and dreams a reality, claiming top victories in a white-dominated sport.

Our girl Audrey knew a thing or two about overcoming adversity, as well. Before making her way as a prima ballerina and becoming one of the greatest female stars of all time, Hepburn was a World War II survivor. During the Nazi occupation of the Netherlands, she saw countless atrocities, including the execution of her own uncle and cousin. Her family was forced to resort to making flour out of tulip bulbs to bake cakes and biscuits. But rather than becoming bitter she said, "Our past has made us what we are today." She went on to say, "Your soul is nourished by all your experiences. It gives you baggage for the future and ammunition if you like."

If at this point you're thinking, "Well, what if I haven't been through the Olympics of suffering? Can I still be successful if I'm the epitome of middle-class suburbia and my mom drove me to school every morning in an SUV?" Of course! One of my good friends, Susanne, is a prime example of a child of privilege who wanted for nothing growing up. Her parents bought her a brand-new car when she turned sixteen (and subsequently, every birthday or special occasion that warranted a new vehicle), and she's never had to pay back a penny in student loans. I typically loathe people like this, but she has never taken her advantage in society for granted. She has volunteered at a battered women's shelter three days a week for as long as I've known her and used to babysit the nursery kids at church every weekend for free. She is a great example that anyone can develop a strong work ethic and moral fiber, regardless of background.

We may already know what it takes effort-wise, but the trickiest step in all of this is getting that first job. Blame it on the day job, but I've heard lots of great stories of how people got that first foot in the door in the music industry, and many times it takes creativity and sheer providence. My friend Jill was a waitress at a nice restaurant one of the record label's executives liked to frequent. She ended up waiting on him several times, and he was so impressed with her service and attention to detail that he offered her a job at the company the next time an opening came up. Another one of my friends, Anne, used to be a sales associate at a little boutique in the mall for a few years before a well-known country music singer started frequenting the store. Anne offered to help her pick out several outfits for her upcoming music video shoot, and after falling in love with Anne's attention to little details and eye for style, the singer hired her to be her personal stylist. Another now-famous country singer landed his first job at a record label in the tape copy room (FYI, not the most glamorous of positions) and would work on his demo tapes there in his free time. One day, a man from the A&R department overheard him playing his songs and offered him a songwriting deal, which eventually launched his career in music. You never know what opportunities may arise when you are faithfully serving at your current situation to the best of your ability. It gives new meaning to the old saying "Bloom where you are planted!"

I have no doubt that there are dozens of other stories like that, from all different industries. The bottom line is that it takes persistence (not crazy-obnoxious-stalker persistence, mind you) and dedication to get to where we want to go. Perhaps you've already laid that groundwork, and after relentless networking, sending out dozens of résumés, and cold-calling everyone and their dog, you finally hear back from a prospective employer—you've got an interview. What a ridiculously frightening process. And unfortunately, the only way to get better at it is to practice. In addition to reciting your interview answers in the bathroom mirror, use this top-ten list of helpful interview hints to make sure you actually get the job.

Top Ten Ways to Get Hired

10. Plan on being at least ten minutes early. Something will always go awry, and you'll be thankful for the extra time; worst-case scenario, you'll just have to wait a few minutes.

9. Dress conservatively—no fishnets, miniskirts or push-up bras—unless, of course, you're applying to be a hooker.

8. Read up on the company's history and be familiar with the job you're applying for.

7. Maintain eye contact—it shows confidence and assures them you're paying attention.

6. Have extra copies of your résumé on hand.

5. Prepare two or three questions of your own to ask (just not about salary, yet)—it shows that you're genuinely interested and invested in the position.

4. Practice a "What are your strengths and weaknesses?" answer. This is a pretty standard question, but it still trips everyone up.

3. Be honest—did you get fired from your last job? Not complete college? Commit a felony? Be upfront and truthful when they ask about life details.

2. Practice being well-spoken—no slang and no swearing.
1. Spit out the gum. Nothing says Valley Girl more than a big wad of Bubblicious!

So, you worked your butt off and finally landed your dream job. (Okay, so the six-by-six-foot cubicle isn't *really* your dream, but you're closer than you were before, right?) You're finally able to throw some of that grocery-store sushi in the cart along with your ramen noodles, and your parents are temporarily satisfied that you have a steady job, "even though your mother and I paid all that money for you to go to school for art history and now you're just working at an online magazine." Things are looking up!

And there's always room for advancement, right? So where do you go from here? Most people say that it's fine to lie on a résumé, because everyone expects it. After all, it can mean the difference between a thousand-dollar cost-of-living raise and having to spend another year in that ghetto apartment, right? And we all know the benefits of leveraging your job, correct?

At first those options seem so sinister and corrupt, but after we've put in two and half years of abhorrent expense reports and late nights at the office, a padded résumé doesn't start to sound half bad! I'm convinced that fluorescent lighting alone could send someone straight to the nuthouse, and after a couple years of that, along with a demanding boss and no payoff, it could very well be the undoing of an entire generation of office dwellers. Like Jim Halpert says on *The Office*, "Right now, this is just a job. If I advance any higher in this company, then this would be my career. And, well, if this were my career? I'd have to throw myself in front of a train." But as much as we might want to go all Miranda Priestly on our coworkers and backstab to get ahead, it's good to know that we do have other options—the best one being extremely simple: just be yourself.

When I first started in the music industry, I felt an enormous amount of pressure to become cold, callous, and crude in order to keep up with the male-driven, tough-business approach. Every time I had a conference call with my peers in the New York office, I almost started crying after I hung up the phone. As much as people would encourage me to toughen up, I couldn't write a demanding letter or make a cruel phone call to save my life. My sweet husband even tried to help and would make me practice writing mean e-mails to him! So I was slightly relieved when I started getting promoted and recognized by just being me, naive pushover qualities and all.

Rita Hazan, celebrity colorist extraordinaire and founder of the renowned Rita Hazan Salon in New York City, says the same thing of when she first started out in her field. "When we hired contractors for the salon, I was involved in it, and I said, 'Hi, I'm Rita.' I learned everyone's name. You don't have to be mean and tough or obnoxious; you just have to be sincere. When people do stuff from their heart, it comes out much better." So, if you're feeling pressure to conform to the industry standards of rude/dishonest/conniving, don't. You can seriously succeed by working hard and simply being your lovely, charming self.

But what if nice goes unnoticed? It seems that the first employees you become aware of in the workplace are the brassy, the obnoxious, and the trashy. You've got about a bazillion brilliant ideas that could revolutionize the company, but somehow the girl with the shortest skirt always seems to get the lead story assignment. If you've got a discerning and intelligent boss, it can never hurt to stop in his or her office, pitch a couple ideas, and show that you're ready to take on more responsibilities.

But maybe you're stuck with a jerky boss who doesn't give a rip about honesty, hard work, and starry-eyed small-town dreams. The higher-ups want movers and shakers and people who yell a lot. One of your greatest resources in this situation is the people around you. If you know you're a future editor in chief, start offering your editing and proofreading services to fellow workers (people always need help with this stuff when typing e-mails, writing out invitations, etc.). Word will quickly get around that you're the queen of lexis, and pretty soon you'll have enough recommendations from everyone in the office to approach someone higher up than your boss. Are you amazing with numbers? Make yourself a human calculator to the ones closest to you, and before you know it you'll have enough references to apply for that accountant position. Do you know that you take better pictures than everyone else put together in the print shop? Offer to shoot weddings, family portraits, and senior pictures for everyone you know, and soon you'll have a portfolio that speaks for itself.

So even if you don't have renowned 'rents or gobs of cash, you can make it happen anyway. In the end, the success will be sweeter, the payoff bigger, the, well, you get the point. Oprah Winfrey, the epitome of achieving big dreams through hard work, once said, "The big secret in life is that there is no big secret. Whatever your goal, you can get there if you're willing to work." Amen to that!

Chapter Four

Choose Your Friends Wisely

"Show me your friends and I'll show you
your future." —*Author unknown*

Thelma and Louise. Paris and Nicole. These were bad relationships. While our friends may not go so far as to help us vacuum up cremation ashes à la *The Simple Life*, there definitely might be room for improvement in some of our friendships. Are you surrounded by gossipers? Compulsive drinkers? Jealous coworkers? Just-plain-lazy roommates? Bad relationships can have a draining effect and dramatically influence us in more ways than we may imagine. And I'd hate to see you drive off a cliff in an ugly scarf just because you couldn't find a decent friend.

First of all, it's no secret that good friends are hard to come by. Just ask Felicity! Keri Russell recently said in a *Self* magazine interview, "My friendships are everything to me . . . as yucky as so many people are, when you find a good one, they're as good as they come. I'm finding a way to find those people." It really does look as if each new day brings new headline stories about Lauren and Heidi fighting, or Nicole Richie and Hillary Duff stealing each other's boyfriends. On the upside of celeb relationships, Courtney Cox-Arquette and Jennifer Aniston maintain their *Friends* bond years later, and Oprah and Gayle still embark on their BFF road trips. But those good-case scenarios seem to be few and far between.

First of all, it's important that we take stock of our current relationships. Are we happy with our friends? Are they dragging us down? Can we count on them no matter what? I'm sure we've all seen enough of *Mean Girls* (or simply lived through the seventh grade) to get a feel for the real damage that bad friends can do. (If only someone would tell Lindsay Lohan to take a real-life objective look at the people she surrounds herself with, she could possibly salvage what's left of her reputation!) But sadly, a lot of us also have an already-established company of liars, partiers, and all-around mean girls—and they may be doing damage to more than just our personal well-being. Because, though we may not think it, we *are* judged by the company we keep.

It's no secret that nowadays future employers are MySpacing potential clients, scrolling through their friend lists and making assessments based on first-mouse-click impressions. (And just for the record, I continue to strongly oppose MySpace and the half-baked girls in halter tops that go along with it!) Those late-night party pics and spring break candids could mean the difference between that assistant editor position and the front-desk gig at the run-down tanning joint on the other side of town. Our posse crashing a work event could mean the end of a job. Even the sororities we belong to could conjure up all kinds of opinions from potential friends and bosses. Honestly, for all I know, Kristin Cavallari could have the IQ of a genius, but because of the laughable bunch I associate her with, I have a hard time seeing her as anything more than a spoiled reality pawn. Our circles of friends have more influence than we think. So, it's best to find a good one.

Relationships in general are a really big deal. Think about it. Life is entirely made up of the conversations, friendships, memories, meetings, fights, secrets, jokes, and experiences we gather from those around us. We come home from work and talk about our interactions with others. We make plans to deliberately leave the house and see specific people of interest to us. When our moms call to check in, they give the status report on our old friends and family members. What would we do without relationships? Who would we share our big news with? Where would we go for a good cry? A friendless life would be a sad existence.

But no one ever told us that starting on the first day of kindergarten we were going to be confronted with many choices of friends, and that the ones we pick could possibly shape our entire existence, so we should be careful. No, friends just seem to happen (at least until later in life, when you're either uprooted by a family move or plopped into a freshman dormitory and forced to become fast friends with the nearest female who likes Dashboard Confessional and bathes regularly). But as we get older and begin making conscious, deliberate acquaintance choices, things get tricky. The friends we choose will be the ones to walk with us through new boyfriends, new jobs, family crises, grad school, weddings, babies, bad breakups, and really bad haircuts. If these "friends" don't support and encourage us, it might be time to seek out some new ones.

How do we go about finding and keeping those really great friends? We can start by surrounding ourselves with positive people. And no, that doesn't mean that you specifically need to run out and make nice with that really perky girl who gets into work at four a.m. every day, or the one at the gym whose ponytail bounces higher than the length of her head. You just need to seek out others who will encourage you when you're having a bad day and, perhaps more importantly, cheer you on when you're having a really *great* day. (I've lived long enough to know that women are perhaps the best species at befriending others when they're down and out and then turning into a jealous bobcat the minute the other one starts to succeed.) A true friend will be there to congratulate you when you win an Academy Award and will also be there to hold your hair back when you're puking your guts out in the bathroom stall two minutes later! So keep your eyes peeled for the hair-holding kind.

As cliché as it may sound, finding someone who's a good listener is also a necessity in friendship. I don't have many pet peeves in life, but one of them is people who can't stop talking about themselves for a minute. Anyone can speak, but it takes intelligence, self-control, and maturity to set our own interests aside and focus our attention on the needs and concerns of someone else for a change. Not only is it hard to feel validated in a relationship where you can't get a word in edgewise, it's just not a lot of fun. A good friendship is built on the mutual sharing of ideas, dreams, concerns, and fears. If we find ourselves on the short end of the sharing stick, it might be difficult to keep the friendship going. And one way we can learn to identify a good listener is by being a great one ourselves.

We can start by asking about our friend's day and then shutting up. We can inquire about our coworker's weekend and then just let them talk about it. Or we can simply stop fiddling with our phones and BlackBerrys long enough to make eye contact and let them know we're genuinely interested in hearing what they have to say. In our drive-up, fly-by, fast-talking society, listening is a lost art. But I'm convinced that we classy ladies can be the ones to bring it back.

The importance of listening also extends beyond close personal friendships—it's a crucial aspect of success. It's no secret that employers relish discovering an employee who does something right the first time, and you can chalk that up to being a good listener. Diane Sawyer even once said, "I think the one lesson I have learned is that there is no substitute for paying attention."

It also doesn't hurt to make the attempt to remember names and faces during introductions and casual meetings. My friend Emily was actually introduced to someone *fourteen* times before he remembered her. Aside from being rude and demeaning, that is just ridiculous. Not surprisingly, Emily was not very interested in pursuing a further relationship with him.

If we're going to go anywhere in life, it's also essential to surround ourselves with friends who have admirable habits and healthy vices. Those who will help us kick our own vices, not just drag us down in the mire with them and theirs. If we're struggling with self-image and potential eating-disorder thoughts (Good Lord, who's not these days?) we need to find ourselves some normal, curvy friends who will take us to counseling and won't care if we're a size 2 or 10. The last thing anyone needs for an on-the-brink eating disorder is another gal pal who just had cardboard and cigarettes for lunch.

If we're trying to get sober, we need to surround ourselves with solid, trustworthy people, rather than our usual group of drinking buddies and bar-hopping cronies. Find a friend who will go with you to AA, or start attending a support group at your local church. When Vicki Vodka comes calling, wanting you to do shots over at her house again, it will be a lot easier to say no when you've got a group of supportive peeps waiting on the other line to go see a movie or eat out at that new restaurant.

Maybe we're just trying to have a better outlook on life. It's easy to get sucked into a negative mind-set when those around us are gossips, critics, and pessimists. Debbie Downer from down the hall will probably not help the situation; we need to seek out optimistic and confident friends who will keep us upbeat. Are we attempting to buckle down and study for grad school? Our usual festivity-planning troupe may thwart our efforts with plastic-cup promises and constant partying. Trying to pay off credit-card debt? We need friends who will be fine with low-budget fun for a while, rather than the usual mall-rat posse. To sum up, we need friends who will support us in our endeavors and, furthermore, friends who will look us in the eye and tell us when we need to get help, rather than simply ignore and even encourage the problem.

In my celebrity-fantasy mind, I like to think that sweet Nicole Kidman encouraged Keith Urban to get help with his drug problem, and just look at how happy and cute they are now with their new little daughter! (I have to restrain myself from racing up and telling them that each time I see them at the Green Hills Mall.) But then there are those obvious cases of people like Amy Winehouse, who choose to surround themselves with leeches who only promote more appalling behavior. It's going to be a vicious cycle of poor choices and even worse consequences if we don't get out of the bad-friend pit immediately.

Of course, that's much easier said than done. Some of these bad friends have been with us for years, and it's hard to simply shake off those relationships. The Queen of Hip-hop Soul, Mary J. Blige, had a similar experience and successfully broke free of her dark past. Of her life changes she says, "I believe environment plays a big part in what happens to you. I was in an environment where nothing was changing and everyone was hanging out with me and drinking, clubbing, and doing drugs with me. The minute something different came in my life and I got a chance to see what it means to be sober, and have confidence in myself, things changed." We can have the same success story; we just need to be brutally honest with our close inner circle and extend an invitation for them to change, as well. Invite them to AA, find new hangouts away from the club, keep each other accountable. It may be difficult for them to understand in the beginning, but after a while, if they don't support our new goals and lifestyle, we can, with no regrets, amicably tell them it's time to part ways.

Besides supportiveness and being considerate, a hefty dose of humor is a key component in any good relationship. If we don't have someone to laugh with about mistakes, boys, and obnoxious coworkers, things are going to get pretty bor-ing. Clearly, I'm no doctor and am by no means offering pre-cise medical stats here, but I have heard that laughter may help stimulate our heart and circulatory system and can actu-ally improve job performance. Perhaps we should all take a ten-minute break from work and just laugh! Our girl Audrey said, "I love people who make me laugh. I honestly think it's the thing I like most, to laugh. It cures a multitude of ills. It's probably the most important thing in a person."

If you need to kick-start the comical in your relationships, check out *I Like You* by Sandol Stoddard Warburg. My two best friends and I discovered this tiny red children's book at a store in New York, and we bought each other copies because it is flawlessly endearing and endlessly entertain-ing. We deemed that each of us could give it away to only one other person in life—the guy we decided to marry. Con-sequently, this humorous little book is sacred among our circle, and I would highly recommend picking up a couple of copies for you and your crew, too.

Another good one to have on hand is *This Book Will Change Your Life* by Ben Carey and Henrik Delehag. After picking it up at a local used bookstore, my college roommates and I almost peed our pants we laughed so hard while reading it. While a bit crude at times, it is a brilliant "daily challenge" guidebook for hysterical everyday living.

Still at a loss for the amusing? The following is a brief

list of entertaining outings and ideas for us and our witty broods to partake in the next time we get bored.

- Buy tickets to see *Spamalot*—sure, Clay Aiken went a little crazy, but the show is still funny.
- Bake cookies with whatever ingredients you have left in the cupboards. I've actually consumed Ramen Chicken Cookies before.
- Buy a $10 kiddie pool at Wal-Mart and throw a pool party. Be sure to invite a designated lifeguard and hang up signs all over that say *No Diving*.
- Rent old episodes of *I Love Lucy*—more specifically, the chocolate-factory episode.
- Get cheap makeovers from the Clinique counter at the mall. Enough said.
- Go to a kids' movie matinee—*Flushed Away* was one of the best movies I'd seen in years!
- Three words: black-light bowling.
- Play Apples to Apples or Taboo—and invite your parents.
- Host a themed party: Christmas in July, Saved by the Bell, the Old West (we required all of our attendees to wear a cowboy hat and boots, and eat baked beans).
- Hit up thrift stores and assemble your next going-out getup entirely from your findings—just be sure to wash them first.

Now that we know what to look for in friends, how do we keep them? I'm sure we've all experienced the friendship that starts out great but then goes to pot after one person moves away, gets hitched, or undergoes a job transfer (all of which are inevitably followed by various promises to "definitely" keep in touch). Or perhaps some of our long-lost friends are still close by but simply too busy to maintain the relationship. I'm still convinced that the best way to keep a good friend is by being the kind of friend we'd like to have. I know we've all heard that phrase a million times, but a little golden-rule action really does go a long way.

As our *Clueless* friend Cher once said, "It's like that book I read in the ninth grade that said, ''Tis a far far better thing doing stuff for other people.'" While her literary accuracy was a little off, the principle still applies. My amazing sister Abby is the absolute best at this. She is hands down the most giving and thoughtful person I've ever met, and she makes me want to be a better friend and human being. One day, she had a bouquet of yellow daisies delivered to me at work, just because! Another time, I came home to a FedEx package on my doorstep—she had found a T-shirt that Rory wore on an episode of *Gilmore Girls* (I'm a little obsessed with that show) and bought it for me just for fun. If we all followed the Abby Practice of Giving, our friends would never leave our side (but we might also be broke).

So what if we're strapped for cash? We definitely don't have to go out and lay down gobs of green to show our friends that we value them; there are plenty of pocketbook-friendly ways to spread the love. A while back, I received a note in the mail from an old friend and it completely made my day, and it only required the chump change to cover the cost of the stamp! Even if you're not a big pen-and-paper person, never underestimate the power of a phone call, a box of chocolates, or even a thoughtful e-mail. (Note: that does *not* include forwarded e-mails. Gross.) We could assemble a recipe book full of a friend's favorite food dishes by simply printing them offline or handwriting some cute recipe cards. And of course, there is still nothing like putting together a good old mix CD (or iPod playlist) to show someone we care. The 1980s love-ballad CD and trashy pop mix that my friends have made for me are some of my favorites to this day.

On the off chance that we do have a couple bucks to spare, we could send a bag of our best friend's favorite candy to work when she gets that raise, or surprise our sister-in-law with a Saturday afternoon of prepaid mani-pedis. Or take a cue from Abby and find quirky paraphernalia from your friend's favorite movie or sitcom. Another great (and cheap!) little gesture is a free-cone gift certificate from Ben & Jerry's. It's also imperative to walk there together and get in some quality talk time. Not only will both parties benefit from the time spent together during a random act of kindness, the act of giving something away seems to elicit a sort of natural high. Audrey Hepburn once said, "It's that wonderful old-fashioned idea that others come first and you come second. This was the whole ethic by which I was brought up."

Another great way to maintain a healthy friendship is having a regularly scheduled date. Even though we lived together, my old roommate and I had a designated ritual of eating popcorn for dinner and watching a movie every Sunday night. We set aside other obligations and assignments and always tried to make that just Blair and Jordie time. And although we work in the same building, I have a standing coffee date with one of my good friends and coworkers, Ruthie. We rarely get to talk about personal things at the office, so it gives us a great excuse to get away for a couple of minutes and catch up on each other's lives. Find a place that works for both parties and make a concrete decision to meet up every week, regardless of outside obligations or circumstances (well, exceptions may be made for emergencies involving oozing blood or exposed internal organs).

Another fun idea to keep the relationship spicy is to set goals together. Two friends of mine, Robin and Whitney, wanted to train for a marathon and decided to run together every single morning (I can say with near certainty that I have not run twenty-six miles in my entire life combined). They consequently developed a close bond and still work out together every morning to this day. Do you have a workout goal in mind? Want to join a gym? Call up a friend/accountability partner—it will make everything way more enjoyable and will force you to keep going and push yourself a little harder even when you're tired.

A couple of my other friends were both trying for acceptance into highly competitive graduate programs and decided to set a daily study goal together. Besides being accepted, they both had a great time and would order takeout and meet at fun, different locations to crack open the books. If you and another groupie are both aiming to get into law school, med school, or just a summer learning program, develop a study schedule together to make sure you're prepped for the LSAT, MCAT, or any other kind of -AT.

If you have several friends who are passionate about the same cause, why not plan an event to raise money and awareness? My friend Kenny loves TOMS shoes, and he personally organized a Christmas party for a bunch of us last year to get together and decorate blank shoes to give to people in need. A couple of my other friends and I support World Vision children, and we always try to brainstorm about new things we can send to "our kids" for birthdays and holidays. Find common areas of passion and ideals with other people and watch those friendships blossom! The basic theory to keep in mind is that if you practice being a good friend to others, the effort will not go unrewarded.

So maybe you're already set in the great-friend department. But if you're anything like me, you always seem to be stuck with a few in your life that you just don't really enjoy. Maybe it's that cousin who called you fat in fifth grade. It could be the girl on the second floor who constantly talks about herself. Or maybe it's that skinny tramp who stole your boyfriend! Either way, you may be forced to salvage some of those (mostly the ones we have to see every day at work), but I've come to the conclusion that some relationships just aren't worth saving. Life is too short to hang around cranky, mean, obnoxious people we don't even really like!

I'll let you in on a secret: I am an innate people pleaser. Consequently, I rarely turn down a request for coffee or lunch . . . or anything, for that matter. One day I realized I was spending thirty-six dollars every week to have burned coffee and small talk with people I didn't even enjoy. Blegh! I generally attempt to be cordial and agreeable, but after months and years of this, it finally dawned on me that I kept going out with these people because I felt guilty, not because I was enjoying it. I started politely declining invitations that didn't involve those that I truly loved and wanted to spend time with, and I realized that I had never felt freer! All of a sudden I was left with spare time to do the things I really wanted to do and found myself wondering why I hadn't cut some people out earlier!

If there's a certain someone you feel not-so-great about spending time with, don't beat yourself up about turning down a social invitation every once in a while. It's your life, which means *you* get to choose your friends. We're all adults here, and if we're finding ourselves investing in acquaintances who aren't contributing to our overall happiness, we shouldn't be afraid to politely excuse ourselves from the relationship. This obviously doesn't have to be a ruthless or cruel process: simply let them know you're busy trying to keep up with the demands of life and need more time than ever to focus on your real priorities. (Ahem, not them. But they don't need to know that.)

Extreme cases of crazy befriending of people are rare, but they do indeed happen. I myself have encountered it only once, and the whole experience practically drove me to drink. Several years ago, a new girl started at work and immediately asked me for my cell number about an hour after she clocked in. I thought that was a little enthusiastic but naively assumed she was just attempting to get to know everyone. She called my cell phone at 6:45 the next morning, asking if I wanted to go get breakfast with her. I knew right then and there that I was not dealing with the average eager beaver.

I politely declined any more early-morning invites and informed her that I, as crazy as it sounded, actually ate breakfast with my husband every morning at home. Later that week, I became slightly concerned when she approached my desk and asked me to buy a gym membership with her. When she called again the next week asking if I wanted to help her make homemade Christmas ornaments, plan a dinner party, and then go for a four-mile hike afterward (I wish I was exaggerating), I knew I had to put the kibosh on the situation.

This part is a horribly difficult thing for me to do, as confrontation is my biggest fear in life. But I felt particularly inspired after watching an old episode of *Friends* where Phoebe and Monica decide to "cut out" their obnoxious friend Amanda, who, among other things, is from Yonkers, New York, but sports a fake British accent and constantly reminds everyone how great she smells and how good she looks. After several requests from Amanda's "mobile," Phoebe gets up the nerve to reject the invite, but Monica cracks under pressure and can't say no to Amanda's obnoxious request to hang out. Overall, their attempt to cut her out doesn't go so well, and they end up having dinner with her anyway. But I'm confident that you and I can be strong and follow through. I finally had to inform Crazy Hiker Breakfast Girl that I had lots of things to juggle between work, family, and freelance writing and unfortunately didn't have time for a lot of outside activities. Luckily, she got the hint and we were then able to peacefully coexist at the office as normal coworkers.

Thanks to Phoebe and Monica, I'm no longer scared to cut people out, and you shouldn't be, either!

Now that we have an established circle of great girlfriends, it's all too easy to get stuck in a rut when it comes to activities. Do we find ourselves going to the same old hangouts? Eating the same Chinese takeout? Watching the same shows every week? My two best friends discovered the perfect cure for relationship-rut blues. We each took a fun online quiz to help us discover our signature cities and made it a point to visit all three of our signature cities before we were out of college. It was the most fun we'd ever had! If you and your gang are up for the challenge, Google "signature city" and "quiz" and have fun!

To further enhance our newfound good-friend habits, here is a slew of out-of-the-box ideas for friends everywhere to enjoy together. This should keep you from being bored for quite some time!

- ❀ Meet at the park for lunch
- ❀ Sign up for hot (Bikram) yoga class
- ❀ Take salsa-dancing lessons together every week
- ❀ Hit up the local farmers' market and make an organic dinner afterward
- ❀ Go see a dollar movie
- ❀ Have a scrapbooking party

- Take a weekend roadtrip to a randomly selected city
- Schedule an old-movie marathon
- Visit an art gallery
- Pick a shopping location and meet up over lunch to window shop
- Buy a disposable black-and-white camera and take random pictures
- Sign up for a cooking class
- Paint each other's bedrooms a new color
- Start your own book club
- Meet up at the local "movies in the park"
- Host a progressive dinner
- Schedule a pedicure together over lunch breaks
- Save up for VIP concert tickets to see your favorite artist
- Take a pottery class and make your own coffee mugs
- Visit an indoor skating rink and brush up on your Ice Capades skills

It's easy to forget just how important friends are until (1) they are gone or (2) they get us into trouble. Actress Rachel Bilson has admitted to having made poor friend choices in the past and talks about what a huge impact it makes on your life. "I had a few years from the age of fourteen till about sixteen when I was hanging out with people I probably shouldn't have been hanging out with, pretending to drink beer and acting cool . . . Then one day, we all got into

a car accident . . . One guy was paralyzed and I was uncon-
scious for a day or two. The accident changed me . . . It woke
me up and stopped me going down that road." Our immediate circle of friends really is much more than just a group to
pass the time with—they can determine our futures.

It's equally important to note that we absolutely need
friends (our good ones, that is). My mom has always been
more than just a mom to me—she's my best friend, and I seriously don't know what I would do without her. I still obnoxiously call her every single day and go over to visit at least once
a week. My sister and I are extremely close, too; I consider her
to be another best friend, and I get seriously sad if I go for
more than a few days without seeing her—and that's the way it
should be, right? Whether or not it's our family that provides
that support system, we just need to make sure we have two or
three close friends we can count on, no matter what.

When we surround ourselves with uplifting and like-
minded comrades, life is just easier to handle. Everything
becomes more fun, and challenges become easier to face. It's
always nice having someone we can call up on the phone for
no good reason whatsoever; someone who won't mind when
we shoot Diet Coke out of our nose from laughing so hard
and someone who'll listen and just let us cry when we've had
the worst day of our life. If we don't have friends like that, it's
time to find new ones—friends who will join us in the pursuit
of living life positively and to the fullest!

Chapter Five

Let Him Come Calling

"It is a truth universally acknowledged, that a single man in possession of a good fortune, must be in want of a wife." —*Jane Austen*

Turns out our mother was right—ladies *shouldn't* make the first move. Let's be honest, do you really want to have to tell your children, "That's right, kids, I had to beat down your father's door and constantly create diversions to get his attention! I sent multiple text messages, wore my shortest skirts, and practically threw myself at him before he noticed me. But don't you worry, I eventually wore him down!" Of course not. We all want a guy to approach us, fall madly in love, and not be able to wait to call us. So how do you make that happen? It's actually not complicated at all (at least not nearly as difficult and convoluted as we girls make it). You'll see how, starting with the basics of dating, the truth about girls who make the first move, the importance of not ruining a good thing, why *he* needs to call *you*, and when it's okay to give it away.

First of all, we live in an extremely deceiving society. We've seen Lindsay Lohan making out with a different guy (or girl) in some pool every week and the Kardashians hooking up with every piece of eye candy the cat drags in. Casual sex is oh-so-glamorous through the lens of movies and TV. Instant messaging, texting, and video messages are the norm between guys and girls. But the painful, real-life truth is that none of this works. Why? Because it goes against the basic laws of nature, that's why! If you glean nothing else from this book, I want you to hear this headline-worthy, urgent-newsflash, critical-emergency, vital-stat message: *We make ourselves waaaay too accessible.* How, you may ask? Let me count the ways.

In no particular order, we have the following means of scaring off a new guy: e-mailing, Facebook messaging, MySpace stalking, texting, calling, showing up unannounced, inviting him over, and did I mention coming on too strong? We will delve into these atrocities in more detail later on and talk about why being so accessible is nothing but a curse, but first let's look at how it ever got to this point.

It's no secret that we girls start fantasizing about a fairy-tale wedding and happily-ever-after love story around the same time we start teething (I still have a wedding book that I compiled at age six!). Relationships are a big deal to us. We want to hear all about our roommate's new boyfriend, have to get every detail of our coworker's upcoming nuptials, and lament right along with Jennifer Aniston over Brad Pitt as if he cheated on us. We love to watch TLC's *A Wedding Story*, feverishly scan *Us Weekly* for the latest blossoming celebrity romance, and sob every time we see *Sleepless in Seattle*. We spend hours prepping ourselves for a date and even more time obsessing about what our potential children will look like and whether or not our initials mesh nicely. Conclusion: girls love love.

So why would you subconsciously sabotage all those efforts through your modern-day attempts at finding true love? This question baffles me daily. I'd like to think that it's out of sheer naiveté—most girls don't appear to be in a lucid mental state when they're throwing themselves at some circus clown off the street and clearly aren't aware that they are actually driving that poor boy further away. But luckily, you will no longer have to be the victim of such careless ways in love, because we're going to start doing things the right way—the old-fashioned way! And it starts by not messing with nature.

Well over a century ago (in 1870, to be exact), William Shakespeare Hays wrote a wonderful song called "Truly Yours." The lyrics just go to show you that this whole love–romance–dating thing has been going on a long time, and we're probably not going to be the ones to change the entire course of it anytime soon.

Truly Yours

'Tis many years since first we met,
When youth was in its prime;
You've made my life a joy to me,—
One long sweet summer time.
Our friendship ripened into love;
My heart but you adores,
And day or night I love but you,
I still am—"truly yours."

Believe me when I tell you true,
Love cannot close its doors,
So long as you are true to me,
And I am "truly yours."

When other lips breathe words of love
And make some promise true,
Then like some swift-wing'd messenger,
My love flies back to you.
Then am I happy, for I feel
Love crushes hearts by scores,
And leaves yours loving noe but me,
While I am—"truly yours."

Though time in its untiring flight,
Teach others to forget,
There's one whose heart you taught to love,
Who fondly loves you yet.
Though I be sitting by your side,
Or off on foreign shores,
Morn, noon, or night, afar or near,
I still am—"truly yours."

In these lyrics we have the entire saga of love and romance summed up in a few phrases: guy meets girl, guy falls in love with girl, guy can't think of anyone but her and is obsessed with girl up until dying day à la *The Notebook*. This age-old plot could explain the rapid popularity of said movie. I know all of us ladies love that love story, and as much as they might grumble, deep down, every guy likes the movie, too (even my husband, who has a beard, drives a truck, and aspires to be a lumberjack). Why? Because it is, without a doubt, the ideal, most picturesque illustration of romance: guys want a girl to chase after, and girls want a guy to want to track them down.

It has always been this way—from Adam and Eve to knights climbing the tower for their lady in waiting to Jane Austen's generation of gallant gentlemen writing letters to their intended, right up to our reality-obsessed era of

Girls Gone Wild. Guys still want to pursue the girl, and no amount of cell phones, sex tapes, and IM conversations are going to change that. I'm not sure why we've all of a sudden taken it upon ourselves to change the structural makeup of a guy's mind, but I'm telling you right now, it's pointless. The implementation of the Sadie Hawkins dance in 1937 didn't do anything to alter the ingrained behaviors of guys and girls. I hate to say it, but you're never going to get the guy until you simply *let him be the guy*. And what do guys want to do? Chase things!

Sometimes it may feel like we are the only ones in this confusing cycle, but this whole process has been around since the beginning of time. It's history. It's nature. It's just the way of it! Men are natural-born hunters—they like the thrill of the chase. It's why boys like to race cars, bid on worthless eBay junk, and go hunting in the woods. They love a good pursuit. You don't see many of us females out tackling opponents to claim some pigskin ball on a perfectly good Sunday afternoon, do you? Nope. We're also not usually on the front lines racing after some impending tornado or disastrous storm. And while we were politely fixing tea and cupcakes for our dolls and friends, the rowdy neighbor boys were in hot pursuit of the bad guy, playing cops and robbers. It's in their nature to hunt, chase, and track down, and if you make yourself readily available (calling, texting, stalking), guys no longer have anything to pursue. And if there's nothing there to chase after, dream about, or hunt down, they've probably already lost interest.

Don't believe me? If you're still of the I'll-get-the-check-not-him mentality, all stubborn and adamant that we just go out and snag a man, I challenge you to take a gander at the responses to the question I posed to ten delightful, successful, happily married men: Did she pursue you, or did you pursue her? Their answers show that the odds are against those trying to muster up the guts to do the asking first.

Jeremy, married five years: I definitely had to pursue Sarah. She wasn't interested in me at all, so I went out and bought concert tickets to see her favorite band to try and impress her.

Herman, married seventy-eight years: I met Emma when I was eighteen and she was just sixteen. I was very nervous about asking her parents' permission to take her out, but I just knew she was the one and knew I had to go for it. So we started seeing each other and were married two months later. That was a long time ago!

Bo, married four years: Even though Claire and I had known each other for years, I had to make the first move. We saw each other for the first time in years, and she just looked so great that I asked for her number and asked her out there on the spot.

Joey, married eleven years: I had to go after Brandi. She just got out of a relationship and didn't really want to have anything to do with me, or any guy, for that matter. But I eventually wore her down, and now she's stuck with me!

Greg, married forty-two years: I had to pursue Carol. Two of our mutual friends even tried to set us up on a date, but she refused! So I just kept asking her out until she finally agreed. We went to a high school basketball game together, and the rest is history.

José, married one year: I had to pursue her. I met Tina when we were playing a show at a small club in this obscure town in Alaska. I thought she was the most beautiful girl I'd ever seen, so I started talking to her after the show, asked for her number, and called her first thing the next morning.

Christopher, married seventeen years: I had to do all the work! I first saw Kerry when our high school football team played her school on a Friday night. She was a cheerleader, she was so cute, and I knew that I just had to say something to her afterward. So I waited around for an hour and a half after the game to talk to her.

Al, married thirty-three years: Well, we were only in eighth grade, but I still had to do the pursuing! I wrote Paula a note, asking if she would go steady. She said yes, and we dated all through high school and got married the day she turned eighteen!

Jefferson, married nine years: I met Bonita at a church picnic and definitely had to pursue her. She didn't want to have anything to do with me, but I just kept annoying her and pestering her until she finally agreed to go on a date.

Ryan, married three years: Natalie came to one of our band's shows with a bunch of her friends; I saw her in the crowd and just knew that I had to go talk to her, so I think you could safely say that I pursued her. I found her afterward, got her number, and haven't stopped talking to her since!

My sweet boy Drew had to do the pursuing, as well—I even turned him down twice before agreeing to a date, because I thought he was too quiet. He told me later that he was beyond distraught and even couldn't eat for days because he knew he wanted to marry me but I didn't seem to want to have anything to do with him! Luckily, he mustered up what dignity he had left and asked again, and as it turns out, the third time was the charm. He ended up taking me to the exact place I had told my sister that I wanted my future husband to take me on our first date, and from that first night on, I knew I was going to marry him, too.

Even rock stars and celebrities have to do some pursuing. When it comes to men being the go-getters in relationships, Kelly Ripa's hunky husband Mark Consuelos says candidly, "I don't think guys like to be put on a pedestal or, you know, have their butts kissed . . . Honestly, that kind of freaks us out. We definitely like a challenge."

When Rob Thomas met his future wife, Marisol, she apparently was not impressed with him or his appearance, and he had to pursue, as well. "He looked awful," she says. "He was wearing khaki drawstring pants he'd rolled up to the knee for some reason. He was also wearing a gigantic T-shirt and a floppy fisherman's hat with Mickey Mouse on it . . . I just thought, 'This is so wrong and so tragic.'" But despite her qualms about his fashion sense, she gave him her number when he asked for it, and a couple of months later, they were engaged.

So regardless of the guy's current status, bank account, background, or beliefs, if he's interested, he will do the pursuing. There's no need to interfere with the ways of nature! Doing so will only scare him off (and I have waaaay too many stories to prove this—ask me sometime and I'd be more than happy to share them!). Of this phenomenon the bold and beautiful Beyoncé says, "When you really don't like a guy, they're all over you, and as soon as you act like you like them, they're no longer interested."

So how do you avoid the clingy-and-desperate act yet still let him know that you're available? It all goes back to not making yourself too accessible. It's not very twenty-first-century-empowered-woman of me to say this, but you simply need to let him call you. Grace Kelly once said, "Emancipation of women has made them lose their mystery." And a woman's mystery is one of the biggest attracting factors for a guy. So when in doubt, just put those phones away and keep them there, because dialing his digits four hours after you've met is only going to turn him off. In fact, here is a list of activities to abstain from during the initial courting period (which can range from the original meeting to several months down the road—you'll know when this time is over when he asks you to be exclusively his!).

■ *Making the initial call*—the only way you're allowed to call him is if he first calls you and leaves a specific message asking you to call him back. There are no exceptions, including "Maybe he lost my number" or "He's really busy, so he probably just forgot" or "He has bad service, so I should just call him." If he was seriously interested in you, he would never, I repeat, NEVER lose that number, and he would easily make his way to some dark alley to get a few service bars on his phone.

■ *Texting incessantly*—especially two hours after you met him to say how much you liked the shirt that he wore tonight. Nothing drains the elusive female mystique faster than a text message that showcases your innermost thoughts and feelings. Leave him to hope, wonder, and get butterflies. Texting does not leave him wanting more.

☎ *Social network interaction*—nothing says overzealous like a creepy MySpace friend request, and I have yet to meet a girl that ended up with a guy she stalked online. If he's interested, he will find you. And even then, you shouldn't get involved in an e-message/IM situation. If he is truly interested, he will want to talk with and see you in person, so there's no need to start a bizarre-o online relationship.

☎ *Too-revealing updates*—you need to completely disregard that impulse to race back to your room and blog that you've just met the man of your dreams. Word will inevitably get back to him that you're obsessed with him, and he'll assume you're a little batty and will be scared poopless. Guys don't want to hear that you're planning their wedding or naming their unborn children (even if you are!), so let's skip the emotional Facebook updates and the tell-all Twitters.

☎ *Planting yourself in strategic spots*—the unnatural act of hanging around his hangouts is not only transparent, it's weird. I'm convinced that if you're truly destined to be with someone, you won't have to leave your house at a calculated time, hide out in the bushes for hours, and then magically materialize, looking fresh-faced, surprised to see him, and very available. For the record, driving by his house or apartment multiple times a day doesn't work, either.

Again, once he has lovingly gazed into your eyes and said that he can't imagine himself with anyone else, you're pretty much free to call and text whenever. Until then, the key is to keep him wanting more. And you can't do that when you're getting a tan from the 24/7 glow of that cell phone, obnoxiously informing him of every minute detail of your day while subtly slipping in hints of matrimony and grand-children. Luckily, by the time he's professed his undying love, it means that he is so enamored of you that you won't be able to get rid of him—soon you'll be politely asking him to just leave you alone for a couple hours so that you can get some actual work done!

One of my favorite literary characters of all time, *Gone with the Wind*'s Scarlett O'Hara, said, "Why does a girl have to be so silly to catch a husband?" Judging by the actions of most females these days, one might think this is exactly what we have to do. Between Tila Tequila's degrading hooker-like antics and the bulk of *The Bachelor* contestants' hot-tub-and-champagne shenanigans, silly is an understate-ment. But in reality, the majority of guys aren't looking for stupid; they just want a fun, smart, down-to-earth girl they can take home to Mom.

Of course, we've all envisioned a happily-ever-after sce-nario countless times. Since the day we hit puberty and started matching up potential suitors' initials with our own on the back of an Algebra I notebook, we were destined for a lifetime of tear-jerk reactions to every emotionally charged life scenario: harsh breakups, timely Valentine's Day card commercials, long-awaited weddings, every sappy movie in the book . . . you name it and we're there bawling our eyes out. And frankly, I think that's just fine.

Romance is part of our female DNA. If you don't believe me, think back on the Disney movies they started feeding us at the ripe old age of two. Although humorous supporting characters helped advance the plotlines, each and every one essentially involved a girl, a guy, and a happy ending: Belle, Ariel, Jasmine, Snow White, they're all just looking for a good man! (My friend Emily is convinced that every one of us has a corresponding Disney princess personality—sheepishly, I took a quiz and discovered that I am Cinderella.) So, at an infantile stage, we're already thinking about Prince Charming (although in some cases he might turn out to be more like the Beast) and wondering exactly how he's going to rescue us, what he'll be wearing, and why on earth he's taking so freaking long to get here. When you add it up, that's a lot of wishing and hoping and praying—from the day we start walking to the day we say "I do!"

Don't be afraid to accept that sentimental and hopelessly romantic fact and simply be a girl and let the guys be guys. There's no use fighting nature, so every once in a while, feel free to give in—pop a bag of popcorn, down a box of chocolates, heck, get a full body massage and manicure.

Don't be afraid to embrace all of that schmaltzy, gooey, lovey dovey-ness. It feels darn good. Sometimes there's only one cure for what ails you—a good chick flick. If you think you've seen 'em all, feel free to further indulge your sappy side and test your cinematic knowledge with the fun quote quiz that follows. Try to guess which movie each quote is from. If you get really stuck, the answers are at the end of the chapter.

1. "I came here tonight because when you realize you want to spend the rest of your life with somebody, you want the rest of your life to start as soon as possible."
2. "A woman happily in love, she burns the soufflé. A woman unhappily in love, she forgets to turn on the oven."
3. "I don't want to put you in a cage, I want to love you!"
4. "This is my one chance at happiness. I have to be ruthless!"
5. "The only things we would've fought about would be what video to rent on Saturday night."
6. "I am nothing special; just a common man with common thoughts, and I've led a common life. There are no monuments dedicated to me and my name will soon be forgotten. But in one respect I have succeeded as gloriously as anyone who's ever lived: I've loved another with all my heart and soul; and to me, this has always been enough."

7. "I was born to kiss you."
8. "You expect me to tell you that you look good? What, did they run out of soap at the Piggly Wiggly since I left?"
9. "That's your problem! You don't want to be in love. You want to be in love in a movie."
10. "There must be something between us, even if it's only an ocean."

Even if you're not a hopeless romantic and haven't been pining away for Mr. Right since you were in diapers, you've probably found yourself baffled by guys and their bewildering actions before. Who hasn't? We've all debated and questioned and reasoned and assumed what's going on inside the male mind. When he fails to call when he says he will, we tell ourselves, "Well, he *is* really busy with work right now." When he says he doesn't want to commit to the relationship, we tend to rationalize, "Well, he's had really rough relationships in the past." And when he can't call or e-mail for two weeks because he's visiting his parents in Idaho, you hear yourself saying, "Well, he is *really* close to his family." But the truth is that we're all big girls and need to stop waiting, groveling, and pining after a doofus who is clearly not interested. You can beg, plead, wish, and pray all you want, but if he's not into it, it's probably never going to happen. Rather than hiking your skirt up an inch higher and cinching your push-up bra an inch tighter, try just reading the signals. The signals are really quite clear, and the more you heed them, the more dignity you'll retain.

At the heart of things, guys are old-fashioned. They want to do the finding, the asking, and the pursuing. If he's not doing any of these and then some, then it was probably over before it began. How do you identify these signals and spare yourself the pain and agony? When in doubt, consult the boy-tested-and-approved list below!

♥ **He doesn't call when he says he will:** I don't care if it's two hours or two days later than when he says he's going to—a guy in love does *not* miss an opportunity to chat with his girl. Period. This pretty much rules out "He might have just lost my number," "He's really busy with work right now," "He has to get up really early," or "He had other plans tonight." Every guy I've ever spoken with (including my own hubby) says that it doesn't matter how busy they are or whom they're with—they'll find a way to call the girl they like.

♥ **He won't commit:** If a guy is in love, he will want to stake his claim. Males are notoriously territorial, and the last thing he would want is another guy moving in on his lady (which should actually make you feel good—you don't want some guy who could not care less if he loses you)! Why on earth would you want a guy you have to convince, bribe, and persuade to be with you? No, thanks. If you've been buying into "He just got out of a tough relationship," "He's trying to figure out his life right now," or "He just doesn't want to do the long-distance thing," you can stuff those excuses in a sack and hit the road, because he's obviously just not interested.

♥ **He doesn't want to move:** He may live a couple of hours away (or in Alaska, Pakistan, or Timbuktu, for that matter), but that absolutely would not matter to a guy in love—he will do whatever it takes to be with the woman he's crazy about. If all this time you've been telling yourself, "Well, he's really close to his family," "He has a really great job there," or "He's just scared to take the plunge," you've been lying to yourself, and deep down, you know it! Guys want to be with the girls they love, end of story. It's really not complicated at all.

♥ **He's not looking for anything long term:** Have we learned nothing from *The Bachelorette*? Guys want to find the love of their life. So if he says he's not looking for anything long term, you can take that as an "I'm just not looking for anything with *you*." It won't do you one bit of good to tell yourself, "Maybe if we just try it for a while, he'll see that we're perfect for each other" or "He's been burned in the past and is just being cautious." When a guy really wants you, he will want all of you, forever. No convincing needed.

So when your Mr. Darcy (or feel free to insert your own favorite fictional male hero here) finally comes along (and he will, mark my words, when you least expect it), how do you make sure he doesn't get away? Leave him wanting more! Contrary to popular opinion, the way to really keep a guy is by not giving it all away. While *Sex and the City* makes a life of one-night stands look glamorous, in reality, it's risky business. Besides making you look cheap and loose, casual sex is confusing and all but dissolves the priceless feminine mystique we possess.

Elizabeth Taylor once said, "I've only slept with men I've been married to." How many women can make that claim? Not many! Besides the looming hazard of unplanned pregnancy (surprise, Mama!), the threat of HIV (not nearly as glamorous as *Rent* portrays it to be), and a host of unpleasant venereal diseases, guys also have no real respect for girls who sleep around. Sure, they'll have their fun for a few nights, weeks, or even months, just because they're guys and they do that kind of stuff, but the chances that he'll be taking you home to meet Mom are slim to none. And if you're on any kind of race-you-to-the-altar timeline, this will only slow him down waaaaay more. Think about it—he's got no need to rush when you're already giving him everything he wants, so why would he be in any kind of hurry to slip a ring on your finger?

I'm still quite unsure of why so many girls are so eager to

toss their "carnal treasure" (thank you, *Win a Date with Tad Hamilton*) in some random guy's face—do they feel that it will seal the deal? Signify that the guy officially likes them? If anything, I would want to make the guy wait for as long as possible to be sure that he does actually like me. Because (I know I said it before, but I think it's worth repeating) if they don't like us without the sex, they're not going to be more interested with it. Just remember that *you* are the ultimate goal, and giving yourself up on the first night leaves nothing left for him to pursue.

To prove that these assertions are not just the ramblings of a madwoman, I'll close this chapter with thoughts from a guy. On his marriage to Demi Moore, the ever-cute Ashton Kutcher says, "It was the smartest thing I've ever done and it took no thought at all. The great things in life tend to be that way." See, we make this way too complicated. If a guy likes you, he will let you know. End of story. Until that happens, you can go on being your classy, witty, and amazing self. When he finally shows up, he won't think twice about asking you out, and all you'll have to do is say yes.

Movie Answers: (1) *When Harry Met Sally,* (2) *Sabrina,* (3) *Breakfast at Tiffany's,* (4) *My Best Friend's Wedding,* (5) *You've Got Mail,* (6) *The Notebook,* (7) *Only You,* (8) *Sweet Home Alabama,* (9) *Sleepless in Seattle,* (10) *An Affair to Remember.*

Chapter Six

Dress to Impress

"A woman's dress should be like a barbed-wire fence:
serving its purpose without obstructing the
view." —*Sophia Loren*

Whether we like it or not, we live in a material world where we are judged by our appearances. In this bizarre, vainglorious land where you've either got it or you don't, we tend to esteem, promote, idealize, and gravitate to those who look the best. (Don't believe me? Did your prom queen more closely resemble Anne Hathaway pre-*Princess Diaries* makeover or post-? Case closed.) For better or for worse, we make entire character verdicts based on the absence or presence of ratty tennis shoes, designer jackets, ill-fitting pants, or leather bags. And knowing that everyone, from guys to potential employers is doing the same with us, we chic, classy girls want to leave a positive first impression with our appearance. But how do we do that?

In our grandmothers' day, you could wear a skirt and stockings or a dress and stockings, but today we have countless options, ranging from the working girl in pinstripes to the drag queen in duct tape. With this anything-goes mentality (don't forget the tattoo sleeves and tube tops!), it's hard to know what exactly is stylish and appropriate. Fashion has become a hodgepodge of styles, and celebrities don't seem to be the trendsetters they used to be. I hate to say it, but 85 percent of the time, you-know-who's red-carpet getup simply looks like thin strips of tissue paper that a parakeet threw up on. If I had the kind of money she does, I think I'd at least try to invest in a flattering knee-length number or something.

Anyway, clothes are still serious business, and we shouldn't be afraid to take them seriously. Looking great involves many factors, including mixing and matching, knowing what to toss and what to keep, and discovering the most important key to *every* outfit (no exceptions!), but it begins with knowing the difference between fashion and style.

In the words of Coco Chanel, "Fashion changes, only style stays the same." While fashion is about flashing lights, runway shows, new designs, and the general pursuit of being en vogue, style consists of our overall presentation and persona—the way that our behavior, ideals, priorities, and personality all shine through in our choices of clothing. Like I said before, it's not about how much money we have to spend. It's about presentation. If we are smart, sophisticated, and chic, our attire will most likely reflect those attributes. On the flip side, all of our rude, grungy, and vile traits can be portrayed through our duds, as well. It's no secret that girls with self-image problems often dress to compensate for the pieces that are missing in their lives. This shows up on the streets daily in the form of blatant bras, fuchsia platforms, and two-inch inseams. Hollywood isn't much better, generally offering up hideous reality shows packed full of scantily clad females with little self-awareness. Like I said before, our level of self-respect shows up in a number of different areas, and fashion, dress, and personal style happen to be some of the biggest and most obvious ones.

Catherine Zeta-Jones says, "I like women who look like women. No one's more feminist than me, but you don't have to look as if you don't give a—you know. You can be smart, bright, and attractive aesthetically to others—and to yourself." As classy, chic, confident ladies, it is vital that we present ourselves as such, and our picks from the closet are the very first thing people take note of when they pass us on the street, meet us in the office, or take us on a date. I personally don't think it's at all out of line to take our clothing seriously. While it may seem frivolous to some, our personal style does more talking than we ever could about ourselves—and we want to make sure it's saying nice things! Just think of all the statements, phrases, and titles that clothes have inspired: "These Boots Are Made for Walkin'," "Off like a dirty shirt," "If the shoe fits," "Lady in Red," "I'm Too Sexy for My Shirt," "Don't get your panties in a twist," and the list goes on.

If we think our attire doesn't have a profound effect on how others view us, we're wrong. Besides our values and standards, we are able to make known our political stance, our emotional state, and even our background and origin, all with our wardrobe. Christina Aguilera proudly waves her "Rock the Vote" T-shirt, signifying her political involvement, Jessica Simpson boldly states her carnivore status with a "Real Women Eat Meat" T-shirt, and Audrina sports a "Little Miss Bossy" T-shirt on *The Hills*. Lawyers wear suits to communicate their professional status, brides wear white to symbolize purity, and beachgoers wear bikinis to show off their bods. We're all sending some kind of message with our clothes. But what kind of message is it? We have the power to come across as self-assured, intelligent, and highly regarded, or slouchy, lazy, and trampy—just by sending silent signals with our personal style. So what is your personal style, and how do you accurately get the classy message across?

Figuring out that personal style is easier than you might think. To find yours, simply circle the five adjectives in the following list that sound the *most* like you.

WHAT'S MY STYLE?

♦ Adventurous	♥ Hopeless romantic	✎ Edgy
👄 Preppy	🚲 Independent	★ Stylish
✎ Mysterious	♦ Daring	♥ Polite
★ Successful	🚲 Eco-conscious	♦ Simple
✎ Entertaining	👄 Organized	♥ Charming
🚲 Free Spirit	♦ Athletic	👄 Classy
★ Passionate	✎ Night owl	♥ Old-fashioned
🚲 Nature lover	👄 Clean	★ Modern
♦ Determined	♥ Caring	✎ Music lover
👄 Put together	🚲 Nonconformist	★ Trendy

Now, out of the five descriptions you circled, add up the number of different diamonds, hearts, lightning bolts, lips, bicycles, and stars beside the traits you chose, and keep reading to match up the quantity you have the most of with the style description!

Mostly Stars ★ You're a trendsetter! You aren't afraid to be the first one to try out a new look, and you're always implementing up-to-the-minute elements in your wardrobe (everything from leggings to headbands). You love to pore over *Elle* and *Vogue* every month, looking for the next big thing in fashion. Style inspirations include Sienna Miller, Rihanna, and Sarah Jessica Parker, and your ideal spots to shop are Bergdorf Goodman and Bluefly.com.

Mostly Diamonds ♦ You're sporty! You love simple, comfortable fashion that doesn't require a lot of extra work, and your ideal shopping trip would be quick and painless. You're always on the go and need an easy, mobile wardrobe that can keep up with you (comfy T-shirts, great-fitting jeans). Style inspirations include Jessica Biel, Serena Williams, and Cameron Diaz, and your ideal spots to shop are United Colors of Benetton and Express.

Mostly Lips 👄 You're classic! You love smart, timeless pieces and are drawn to sophisticated designs and elegant lines and colors. You always look put-together and love to keep your wardrobe updated and organized with classy colors (white, navy, gold) and chic silhouettes (wrap dresses, trench coats, fitted button-ups). Style inspirations include Katie Holmes, Jessica Alba, and Jennifer Aniston, and your ideal spots to shop are J.Crew and Ralph Lauren.

Mostly Lightning Bolts ⚡ You're rock 'n' roll! You love the glam, underground look of music groupies and are drawn to rebellious punk-rock elements (band T-shirts, Chuck Taylors) and bold colors (black, fuchsia, charcoal). You aren't afraid to go against the grain and create your own hybrid rock-meets-couture look. Style inspirations include Ashlee Simpson, Agyness Deyn, and Gwen Stefani, and your ideal spots to shop are Urban Outfitters and Vivienne Westwood.

Mostly Hearts ♥ You're sweet! You love elegant, romantic tops and dresses with subtle feminine touches like lace and ruffles. You look for soft, graceful fabrics and colors (ivory and dusty pink) and simple, pretty pieces (tea-length dresses, blouses with pearl buttons). Your look is understated yet refined. Style inspirations include Kate Bosworth, Natalie Portman, and Nicole Kidman, and your ideal spots to shop are Anthropologie and Nanette Lepore.

Mostly Bicycles 🚲 You're bohemian! You love loose, free-flowing tops and skirts and are drawn to natural fabrics (organic cotton, hemp bags) and easy-to-wear garments in earth tones (brown, burnt orange, olive green). You look for inexpensive pieces you can mix and match. Style inspirations include Mary-Kate and Ashley Olsen, Nicole Richie, and Kate Hudson, and your ideal spots to shop are Buffalo Exchange and local vintage/thrift stores.

Now that you've established your overall style, you can begin to refine and work with your personal look, shaping yourself into a raving beauty! Famed English designer Mary Quant once said, "Fashion is not frivolous. It is part of being alive today." It's true—each and every day we *have* to put something on when we leave the house, so no matter how much we may resist and say that we're not into style or concerned with materialism and trends, we really are taking part in fashion in some way, shape, or form—it's simply either going to look really great or really terrible. So if we have to make the effort anyway, why not make it look great?

Great style starts with always looking your best, no matter what day, time, or occasion. Coco Chanel also once said, "I don't understand how a woman can leave the house without fixing herself up a little—if only out of politeness. And then, you never know, maybe that's the day she has a date with destiny. And it's best to be as pretty as possible for destiny." Who knows what untold glories and fateful encounters each day will bring (or disasters and calamities, which might require hospitalization—for which possibilities my mother always reminded us to put on clean underwear), so we should err on the side of caution and simply look our best at all times. Lord knows that the one time we make a quick run to the grocery store in our high school track team sweatpants and a paint-splattered bandanna, we will inevitably run into our boss or ex-boyfriend.

While people have been thrown out of restaurants and dismissed from parties for being underdressed, I have yet to hear of anyone being asked to leave because they looked too good. Once at lunch, I overheard a work acquaintance talking about a party she had thrown that weekend. She had invited an intern from her workplace, and the poor girl showed up at the formal cocktail party in a cowboy hat and Wranglers. After the ripple of laughter had died down at the lunch table, she explained that she figured the girl's humiliation of having to squeeze by oodles of leather miniskirts and sequined halters on the way to the drinks table was punishment enough, so she didn't ask her to leave. I couldn't help but feel sorry for the inexperienced intern, but it did cross my mind that the whole situation could have been avoided by simply not dressing too casually for *any* party. In fact, it would be much better to be overdressed than underdressed in most social scenarios, including blind dates, job interviews, and meeting future in-laws. People always remember a chic and classy outfit, so when in doubt, dress it up.

It's worth noting, however, that when hosting a bash, it's always best to communicate to guests the expected dress ahead of time in order to avoid such a disaster. They will be grateful for the heads-up and much more comfortable when they show up in the requested cocktail dress rather than their ol' boots and Daisy Dukes. If you are the guest and are worried that your ball gown might be a little much for that upcoming clambake, don't hesitate to ring up the host and inquire about attire—better safe than sorry!

Jane Austen once said, "One man's style must not be the rule of another's." We may not all be able (or want) to traipse around every day in Audrey's signature sleeveless dress and kitten heels, and that's fine by me. As we found out earlier, though each of us has a different style, we can all attain a look that is smart, classy, and fashionably us. Assuming that none of us have the disposable resources of Melania Trump, the key to developing that stylish and classy wardrobe is the art of mixing and matching. If you're like me, you've got a few key pieces that are beyond fabulous and, unfortunately, cost more than monthly rent. While they may be exceptions, they are without a doubt the items that we receive the most compliments on and make us feel like a million bucks. So while we may not be able to lay down eight hundred smackers every month for a new pair of Christian Louboutins, we can successfully pair our spectacular splurges with a few economical pieces.

For you trendy stars, don't be ashamed about a few great purchases like knee-high boots (to tuck your skinny jeans into, of course), a cropped, fitted leather jacket (D&G is pretty much the be-all, end-all), and a bag that makes everyone jealous (my Tano has held up under extreme conditions and still gets rave reviews daily). Just be sure to fill in the gaps with affordable side items like tank tops from Old Navy, aviator sunglasses from UrbanBoundaries.com, and a bartered watch from Chinatown.

If you're a sporty diamond, fashion splurges probably don't come easily. But don't be afraid to go for broke on a perfect, tailored pair of jeans (Earnest Sewn will customize), a cute hoodie that's not overly athletic (check out Gypsy 05), and a great pair of flats to keep everything feminine (J.Crew has a multitude of brilliant new patterns and colors each season). Then you can pinch your pennies by stocking up on capri yoga pants from Target, earrings from Claire's, and a baseball hat from your favorite team's Web site.

I know I don't have to beg the classy lip girls to indulge in a few nice pieces, because my sister is pretty much the "classy" poster child, and she could easily drop $500 on a silky head scarf without batting an eyelash. But specific pieces to concentrate on are timeless articles like a great pearl necklace, a black wrap dress (can't get any better than Diane von Furstenberg), and, yes, maybe even a pair of Jimmy Choos. (As my friend Kristen says, "Life is short. Buy the shoes!") But be sure to give your credit card a rest with a few lower priced purchases like plain, stretchy tees from the Gap, dress pants from Ann Taylor Loft, and a clutch from Hobo International.

For rocker lightning bolts, treat yourself to a pair of black suede ankle boots like Franco Sartos, a great printed tank by Lauren Moshi, and a flirty dress from Betsey Johnson for that upcoming wedding. Mix and match with less expensive necklaces from Target, band T-shirts from Urban Outfitters, and a girly-ruffles-meets-rock-'n'-roll Franchi handbag. You will absolutely be the envy of everyone at the show.

If you're a sweet and dainty heart girl, shopping is easy with so many cute new products and designs out on the market. Go ahead and break the piggy bank for a neutral skirt that goes with everything (try BCBG), a wonderful pair of kitten heels (Anthropologie's are adorable), and a fitted jacket, preferably with ruffles (Sunner and J.Crew both have great options). Save on simple pieces like lightweight tops from H&M, cardigans by Free People, and cotton sateen dress pants from Banana Republic.

For bohemian bicycles, we can get in touch with our inner materialist and pick up an organic-cotton knee-length dress by Linda Loudermilk, a big boho-chic bag (Noon Solar has one that charges your cell phone or iPod on the go using solar power!), and a go-to cardigan (check out White + Warren's duster cardigans). We can save our remains for a rainy day with economical pieces like comfy ballet flats from Gabriella Rocha, wide-leg jeans from Guess, and a stack of copper bangle bracelets from Claire's.

Now that you're mixed and matched, the next key to looking classically and stylishly great is buying things that fit. Stacy London, cohost of TLC's addicting style phenomenon *What Not to Wear* (on a side note, my sister and I are kind of in love with Clinton Kelly), says, "Women have a tendency to squeeze into things and say, 'If I buy this, there will be motivation for me to lose weight.' Then, when that doesn't happen, the skirt hangs in the closet as a shameful reminder. Tugging at your clothes is never a good look." I am personally guilty of this, and you might be, as well. Rather than packing ourselves into a size too small, let's just buckle down and buy what fits us now. If we don't, we may find ourselves the targets of comments such as, "They look like ten pounds of poop stuffed in a five-pound bag" (insensitive remark compliments of my husband).

To avoid getting caught in the wrong size, you should always try everything on. If you're really uncertain about the exact fit, take a friend along to the dressing room and ask for brutal honesty. I think we're all well aware by now that there is no such thing as consistent sizing. So if you're regularly a tiny 2 and have to pour yourself into an 8 at Abercrombie, don't feel bad (you can explain to me later why you're even shopping there in the first place.) Likewise, if you're a standard 10 and suddenly find yourself slipping into a 4 with ease, you should stock up on one in each color and keep that blissful feeling going every day! The key is buying items that fit us *today*—not things that will potentially fit five months down the road after our stint with Weight Watchers.

Never underestimate the power that colors, prints, and fabrics play in flattering your shape. While I'm all for mixing fashion with fun, it's safe to say that a pair of fuchsia pants might not flatter our rear ends quite as well as a sleek black or charcoal pair. Crazy graphic prints also have their place, but bear in mind that it may be at the expense of your slim silhouette. When in doubt, a solid color is always a safe bet—just make sure it isn't a solid *neon* color.

Even certain fabrics like corduroy and wool can have an

effect on our appearance—and not necessarily in a good way. One of my favorite items of clothing is this huge, lumpy brown sweater that undoubtedly adds ten pounds to my physique. As much as I love that thing, I try to limit its appearances in public, as it makes me look like a fat angora rabbit. On the contrary, extremely skimpy fabrics can have just as much of an adverse effect, showing every unpleasant ripple of flesh and patch of cellulite we've got tucked away. Look for fabrics that complement and highlight your figure rather than drowning it or, worse yet, turning it into a tell-all memoir. Yikes!

We've all seen unfortunate bodies at the beach—ones that have no business whatsoever even being close to a two-piece but are strutting around in bikinis cinched so tight you'd swear the wearers' eyeballs were about to pop out. Or there's the token girl out on the town in a skirt that's too short, a top that's too small, having a drink that's too strong—never a good combination. And of course, we've all skimmed the mortifying *Glamour* Don'ts and witnessed a multitude of saggy pants, mismatched separates, loose tops, and ill-fitting shorts. Truth be told, we've probably all been a *Glamour* Don't at some point in our lives, but as long as we can objectively recognize our areas of style weakness, we can begin to choose the right things for our body type—nothing that bags, sags, bunches, pulls, or requires immediate assistance.

One way to avoid such mishaps is by custom-fitting every-thing. If this were 1876, we could all just stay home with our sewing kits and turn out oodles of custom-made clothing, but I'm going to guess that most of us don't spend much time with the ol' needle and thread anymore. So while it's probably a little too much to ask that we all give up our day jobs to make our own clothes, we *can* befriend a tailor or seamstress. Alterations don't usually cost nearly as much as you would imagine, and some stores even offer custom fit-ting, measurements, and alterations for free. J.Crew offers the service gratis on all full-price items, the Buckle will hem jeans and make minor repairs on other items, Ralph Lauren does complimentary alterations on full-price Collection apparel, and Banana Republic makes free tweaks for luxe house credit card holders. Some department stores, like Nordstrom, also offer the service. Just make sure to ask for an employee who is specialized in the alterations area; other-wise those business-suit trousers could come back looking like pedal-pusher toddler pants. Getting a great tailored fit to our clothes can make all the difference in the world. As Victoria Beckham says, it's "that extra half an inch!"

Now, if you've so much as stepped outside your door in the past four years, you'll know that modesty and tasteful dis-cretion are no longer the name of the game. It can be intimidating and discouraging when we've got Heidi Montag and her false assets spilling out of every tank and tee, and Lindsay Lohan high-stepping it down the red carpet in the shortest skirts known to man, but let's be honest, those looks aren't flattering on anyone. While it can be tempting to want to keep up with the current inseam trends, the respect we'll receive from *not* exposing our chest region and upper thighs is worth so much more than the five-second stares we'd get from a bunch of ogling buffoons.

Modesty and sophistication are still stylish virtues, and although we don't have the current influence of golden girls like Audrey, Grace Kelly, or Princess Diana on the red carpet or in magazines, a handful of existing A-listers, like Mandy Moore, Raven Symone, and Alexis Bledel, make modesty look hot. Another girl who always looks radiant without flashing everything to the world is Carrie Underwood, who recently said, "I definitely don't do stomach, because nobody wants to see that. I'd be pulling at my clothes all night. You can be intelligent, sexy, and not have boobs everywhere." The smart and well-spoken Megyn Kelly also finds modest ways to still look gorgeous while delivering the daily headlines on Fox News's *America's Newsroom*. She says, "I object to seeing any armpits on air. I don't need to see that." Indeed, I would argue that a few cleverly concealed areas are much more attractive and sexy than exposed midriffs and cheeks . . . and I'm not talking about the ones on our faces!

To purge the closet of all potentially slutty items, consult this handy What to Keep, What to Toss chart to learn which pieces to hang on to and which to burn, according to personal style, of course.

Style	What to Keep	What to Toss
☆	Vests, belts, boots	Skimpy clubbing halter top and anything that exposes the midriff
♦	Yoga pants, hoodies, baseball hats	Free T-shirts and any skirts that don't reach at least midthigh
👄	Jewelry, suits, jackets	Old pairs of Keds and low-cut numbers that show cleavage
⚡	Leather jacket, classic band shirts	Converse tennis shoes and all articles of clothing with cigarette burns on them
♥	Pearl necklace, dresses, heels	Faded, colorless tops and lumpy, ill-fitting bras
🚲	Long skirts, bags, scarves	Shoes with holes in them and paper thin, see-through spaghetti-strap tanks

One of the other secrets of cute-but-modest dressing is the art of layering. Starting with our bum (and assuming that none of us wear mom jeans yet), we probably all struggle with the whole low-riders-and-underwear-showing thing. The best way to remedy this without throwing away all of our Seven jeans is through the use of camisoles. Victoria's Secret actually has a really great selection of long ones that tuck effortlessly into jeans and keep our undies from being exposed to the world (and as a bonus, our midriff in front). The slim layer of fabric doesn't add bulk to the outfit and actually seems to create a somewhat slimming effect by keeping everything sucked in!

When it comes to our bottom half, it's best to save short skirts/bare legs for the beach and take advantage of layering assets such as boots, jeans, tights, and leggings. Not only are layered pieces flattering, they cover up razor cuts, unsightly bruises, and five-inch childhood scars. Plus they're just fun. Not to mention the fact that it takes an incredibly high level of maintenance to prep and expose our gams to the world (shave, exfoliate, lotion up, spray tan, repeat), and I don't know about you, but even then, mine still never look that good, as much as I like to imagine ZZ Top singing "Legs" as I leave my house in the morning. So while light Bermuda shorts are great options for spring and summer and pencil skirts are still good for our stems during fall and winter, let's skip the hip-to-ankle exposed skin and add a couple of layers.

Then, of course, there is the art of layering on top. If ever in doubt about whether or not a top is boob-friendly, simply face a mirror and bend directly over—can you see anything? If not, you're golden. If it's cleavage-city, you may need to call for backup. While there's no need to go to the extreme of slipping an unsightly dickie on underneath every top à la Cousin Eddie, a light camisole will do the trick and works great for keeping the girls from being spotted. Adonna makes a good long-enough-to-tuck-in cotton undershirt that's also high enough to keep anything from popping out. And it's light enough to not add bulk to the rest of an ensemble.

There are countless benefits to dressing cute but modestly, including the fact that you don't have to constantly worry that a slight wardrobe malfunction could mean a citation for indecent exposure. A simple act like climbing out of the car won't expose your crotch to the universe, and one missing button won't be the downfall of your entire top. It will even make you feel more classy and confident. And you'll garner respect from your reputable wardrobe—fellow females will take you out to eat, employers will take you seriously, and guys will want to take you home to meet Mother.

Though they're usually finishing touches, it's the little clips, straps, tapes, and pins that make all the difference in the world. Granny panties, purple silkies, double-sided tape, boulder holders, skivvies, clear straps, strapless see-through, underwires, boy shorts, pushups, garters, shapers, slips . . . we girls have got a lot of things going on under there. The

Changing Times called them "Unmentionables—those articles of ladies' apparel that are never discussed in public, except in full-page, illustrated ads." It's a full-time job keeping everything in place, and anyone who says differently is lying! Growing up in my family, the weekly Sunday morning ritual of getting ready for church was nothing short of sheer pandemonium. Three girls attempting to get everything tucked in, glued on, and pinned down at the same time always resulted in a small cyclone of hosiery, spandex, curling irons, and bobby pins—all followed by a thick fog of Vavoom hairspray, of course. Oh, the trials we endure to look good. Whoever says that girls have it easier has clearly never tried to put on a body slimmer!

We probably all have horror stories of things falling out, slipping up, or coming unglued, and these disasters can ruin an entire evening. English singer Sarah Harding said, "This is awful. I was feeling really glamorous in the dress and now I can't even bear to think about what happened," after accidentally exposing her thong. Visible bra straps, in-your-face thongs, and unobstructed boobs are the last things we want showing when trying to up the class factor, and there are several good rules of thumb to avoid just such a calamity.

First of all, everyone should know by now that it's just never a good idea to go without underwear, especially if we're planning on crawling out of a low-rider vehicle surrounded by paparazzi. If we decide to go with a subtle, panty-line-less thong, we need to make sure that our pants and shirt are conducive to such a decision. And as mentioned earlier, many times, if our underwear is consistently peeking out of our half-inch inseam jeans while we're out for a casual stroll, we may need to invest in a long camisole to take care of the thong-sighting threat. Nothing says trashy like a pink whale tail poking out of a classy, stylish outfit.

Second, if you can't walk in it, ditch it. If one heel in a gutter is going to send you keeling into the street, you might need to rethink the skin-tight python skirt. Or if one lean forward propels the girls directly out of that top and into the eyes of an innocent onlooker, you may need to change into something less constricting. I actually knew a girl whose boyfriend went shopping with her when she would try on shirts, and he would make her bend over to make sure no one else would be able to see her boobs in it! I still haven't decided if that's sweet or creepy. Bras also have a tendency to peek out from gaps between those two buttons right around our bustline if a shirt is just a bit too tight, creating a nice peep show for the guy across the board room conference table. However, that problem is easily remedied with a good ol'-fashioned safety pin (thanks, Mom!) or double-sided tape designed for clothes.

Lastly, nothing is more frustrating and anxiety-inducing than the panic of realizing that a button is missing. A strap broke. A seam came unraveled. We dart to the bathroom and are forced to rig up every kind of makeshift loop, holder, and pin possible from nothing but the contents of our clutch and the bathroom janitor's supply closet. My sister is an amazing seamstress and can fix up anything on the fly, but if we're not so lucky (and can't manage to get the soap dispenser lever or tampon string to hold up our skirt), we should always try to have a safety pin on hand. Those little guys can fix almost anything and can be effortlessly toted around in our bags. If you want to go all out, invest in a little five-dollar sewing kit from the drugstore to keep in your purse, as well—they're tiny, handy, and extremely cute.

Above all else, there is *one* fashion accessory that should complement every outfit, every day, with no exceptions: a smile. Lee Mildon once said, "People seldom notice old clothes if you wear a big smile." So true; we don't have to have the latest designer duds to come across as warm and appealing. On the contrary, no matter how gorgeous the subject or how fabulous the outfit, if they're not enjoying themselves, it's wasted. As striking as she is, we rarely see Kate Moss crack a smile, and I think it affects her overall appearance. On the other hand, Heidi Klum is always glowing and bubbling over with joy and energy and genuinely appears to be loving life, which I think adds to her already beautiful demeanor. A smile is *always* the cherry on top of any great ensemble, and we shouldn't leave the house without one. Jenna Lyons, senior vice president of women's design at J.Crew, agrees: "This is the most important rule. It is so much harder to be critical of what someone is wearing when she is lovely, connected, and interesting." A smile can cover up a multitude of sins, including bad hair, bad shoes, and bad clothes, so if you should happen to get caught looking not-so-good, just flash your pearly whites.

I have embarrassing proof that a smile can counteract clothing woes. Once in college, I tucked myself into bed early on a Wednesday night, only to be awakened by a phone call from a friend two hours later.

"Hey we're all down at 12th and Porter, and your favorite band is playing!"

Now, I was tired, groggy, and slightly miffed about the rude awakening but decided to drag myself out of bed anyway, mumbling that I would probably regret it later if I didn't go. Without thinking, I threw my hair in a ponytail and made my way down to the venue in nothing but my Lynyrd Skynyrd T-shirt, Paul Frank pajama pants, and wool toggle coat. Once there, my friend introduced me to a "new guy." Mortified by my slumber-party ensemble, I decided to compensate by being overly confident and smiley. We started chatting, and he ending up asking me out! Monkey pants and all. Granted, I certainly wouldn't recommend donning footie pj's for any event, and I fully realize that I blew my own rule of "always look your best," but my experience that night underscored that if you're ever caught without the right ensemble, it's best to grin and bear it.

If you're doing everything you can to keep your duds classy, your appearance appealing, and your smile big, you'll see results immediately. Boys will come calling, fellow females will want to know where you shop, and your employer will take note of the distinct difference between you and the rest of the sloppy workforce. You won't have to worry about ending up in the *Glamour* Don't section or looking like you could top a worst-dressed list, and you certainly won't have to worry about accidentally flashing your goods to the free world just by stepping out of the car.

Clothing is so much more than just the threads we throw on our backs every day—it directly expresses our values, persona, and self-image. We all see girls at work, on the street, and in the tabloids who have poor self-image and clearly feel the need to compensate and strip down to the bare minimum, hoping and begging for attention. But we are not dumb, desperate, or void of self-respect, and don't need to sport a scandalous top or questionable skirt anytime soon. We represent the exact opposite—we smart, sassy, and radiant girls know what we want and refuse to let a run in our hose keep us down! Let's begin dressing like the stylish and sophisticated dames we are and represent the next big thing in fashion—class!

Chapter Seven

Less Is More

"I don't think makeup is rocket science or a
cure for cancer." —*Cindy Crawford*

Sandra Bullock once made the insightful declaration, "Makeup is scary." I couldn't agree more. While walking into Sephora is indeed exhilarating and glamorous, it can be overwhelming (especially to those of us who wore nothing but mascara and ChapStick up until college). But according to today's bigger, better, over-the-top mentality, the ones who spend hours on their hair and makeup get all the attention, and we gape aghast at women caught running to the supermarket or yoga class in nothing but aviators and a hair tie. Personally, I am always delighted to see Heidi Klum foundationless and Reese Witherspoon sans her lip gloss. Most women are flawless *without* makeup and look absolutely perfect in their natural state, but we have somehow been deceived into thinking that it's absolutely necessary to join the ranks of the facially plumped-up, thinned-out, and overdone. Not anymore! It is entirely possible to look pristine without packing on the products. And one of the first steps to recovery is admitting there's a problem.

A fellow student-council representative in high school mainlined Mary-Kate and Ashley products. I swear, from the first waking hours of the day to the final fleeting moments before bedtime, she would apply layers upon layers of purple Shimmer Plus Eye Shadow. While I wasn't quite sure of the reasoning behind this, I admired her obvious preparedness to hit the clubs at nine a.m., should the opportunity have presented itself.

Once, I caught her on an off-day while she was frantically applying the primary coat of varnish in the bathroom mirror at 7:15 a.m. After I got over the initial shock of seeing the girl minus her usual layers of molded wax, we started discussing the upcoming pep-rally efforts, and I silently absorbed her whole thirty-five-minute ritual. As eyebrows were shaped and clouds of beige powder foundation filled the air, I speculated, *Who in the heck is she doing this for?* The length of the routine seemed appropriate for only two things—a Broadway actress on opening night, or a showgirl in Vegas. I had seen the washed-up, male miscreants who attended our school and they certainly weren't worthy of this caliber of aesthetic application. And she had an established group of nice friends who weren't really the vain, judgmental type. So after we covered the concession stand donations, I cautiously broached the subject.

"I don't think I've ever seen anyone put on that much makeup," I stated in my best nonchalant tone.

"Well, I look really horrible without it. So I have to," she answered somewhat matter-of-factly.

Let's stop right there. It's bad enough that we have been brainwashed into thinking that we *have* to wear makeup, but to feel the additional need to start caking it on at seven in the morning during high school is just plain sick. (I'm a little out of touch with the elementary school crowd, but I swear I saw a fifth grader sporting false lashes and lipstick at the grocery store the other day—*that*, my friends, is frightening.) Our society is undoubtedly of the flashier/louder, faster/stronger mentality, and for some reason, makeup tends to fall into that same category, but it really should be placed indefinitely in the less-is-more category. The student-council girl was very attractive and likable—she certainly didn't *have* to wear makeup. And in fact, none of us do. We need to realize that makeup is simply something to enhance certain features—not a daily necessity that needs to be applied from sunup to sundown.

World-renowned cosmetic industrialist Helena Rubinstein once said, "Whether you are sixteen or over sixty, remember, understatement is the rule of a fine makeup artist." Yes, despite the obvious superficial, psychological, and emotional benefits makeup offers, it has the tendency to be really over-done. So how do you get a beautiful glow without looking like Courtney Love dipped in Crayola? We can start by differentiat-ing between the need for a big-screen-ready red-carpet make-over and the beautiful simplicity of everyday application—we need to *use the contents sparingly.*

We all know that foundation is more or less a small vat of miracles and that nothing feels more bold and sexy than slathering on a big coat of red lipstick, but like anything else, there can be too much of a good thing. If you don't believe me, hit up the nearest Glamour Shots booth at the mall and report back to me with your findings. If you can get past the racks of feather boas and neon backdrops, you're bound to get hit in the face with a tube of fuchsia sparkle gloss or a gallon barrel of blue eyeshadow at some point. While you may not have stooped to that level of excessive application, you may be inadvertently covering up some of your best features.

Another leading lady of cosmetics, Lauren Hutton, once said, "That's the mistake women make—you shouldn't see your makeup." Do you have a mole or beauty mark? Let it stand out as your distinguishing feature! How about full, pouty lips? Don't play them down! I realized I was doing this very thing one day when a friend said to me, "I can't see your freckles anymore. I think they're cute and it's kind of sad to see them covered up." I have secretly always enjoyed my Amber-Valletta-esque dusting of cheek freckles and was taken aback to learn that I had been covering them up every day with foundation and concealer. We can avoid such disasters by simply applying the bare minimum. There is a time and a place for heavy makeup, and that time and place isn't usually every day! Don't be afraid to let your unique and distinctive features shine through.

Another great way we can look our best is by remembering an old cliché: "the difference is like night and day." Until I witnessed one of my acquaintances prancing around our college campus in full-on club makeup after our nine a.m. class, I had never realized the importance of distinguishing between day makeup and night makeup. I know we've all seen big-haired, full-lipped ladies out and about during lunchtime, looking as if they just came from their gig as rodeo clowns. Or maybe it's the new assistant from downstairs who looks to be fully prepped for Boy George's birthday party during an eight a.m. meeting.

To save face (all right, pun intended), skip the heavy liner during the daytime and simply dab on some toned-down eyeshadow and a few coats of mascara. You can also just apply some tinted lip gloss for the office and save the liner and thick lipstick for dinner out on the town later. Also, rather than going for full-on blush during the day, simply sweep a little bronzer around your face and neck to avoid looking like death warmed over. Dark colors and thick products tend to weigh the face down, so using lighter tones and minimized amounts will keep us looking fresh and awake during the day. Using the contents sparingly will help you with maintaining that airy, luminescent, Glinda-the-Good-Witch glow until you leave the office, rather than melting into one big pool of black liner by four p.m. like Almira Gulch in front of a heat lamp.

A bonus to using night makeup at the appropriate time is the thrill of being able to play with fun colors that we wouldn't typically wear. Half the pleasure of getting ready for a special occasion is adding some va-voom to our usual makeup routine—darker eye shadow, liquid liner, big lashes. But if we're continually sporting our night makeup all day long, then there's no place to go from there to amp things up a bit! I had a friend at work who wore her full face day in and day out, and she often bemoaned how sad it was getting ready for weddings and parties: "Everyone else looks so great when we go out, but I look exactly like I do every single day! I can't do anything more with my makeup!" There should be a distinct difference between our big-event veneer and our everyday look.

If that isn't enough reason to make you turn in your wands and liners before noon, the prospect of a guy certainly always will! Besides scaring the poor barista at Starbucks during your morning coffee run, gobs of out-of-place makeup can be intimidating to boys. Yes, men as a whole may be attracted to Pamela Anderson, but I've had several guy friends tell me that girls with tons of makeup simply gross them out. In fact, a guy I work with actually told his wife that he liked her better with little to no makeup because she was just naturally pretty and didn't need any.

Once while I was home sick, I took in a little program called *Confessions of a Matchmaker.* (I can already hear the sighs and groans of judgment, but it really was entertaining!) The host, Patti Novak, set up a too-much, too-tight, too-tan girl with a sweet, down-to-earth guy in hopes of breaking the girl's bad track record of scaring off guys. Patti described the girl's look as harsh and fake, rather than bold and sexy, and she advised her to tone down her excessive makeup and lay off the tanning bed for a few days. Of course, our young dater didn't heed Patti's sage advice and showed up to dinner with her pink-flamingo press-on nails a-flashing and her denim mini riding up to high heaven. She was forced to keep her eyes half open at all times in a creepy, bulging kind of way because of her too-thick false lashes and eye goop, and she was, of course, teetering on the edge of disaster all evening in her five-inch stilettos. Not surprisingly, at the end of the evening, the sweet boy dropped her off early and kindly informed the camera that she may have been a nice girl, but looked absolutely ridiculous and simply *wore too much makeup.*

Yes, despite our best attempts to lure the opposite sex with smoky eyes and dramatic lips, it might all be just a bit too much sometimes. Guys are more perceptive than we give them credit for, and generally, a mug covered in clown paint comes across as someone desperate, unapproachable, or just plain smutty. We want the world to see us for the classy, intelligent girls that we are, so let's not ruin it with an overabundance of bronzer and glitter gloss!

Going against the popular trend of "Don't like it? Fix it!" we also need to learn to work with what we've got. While many celebrities are quickly becoming poster children for plastic surgery (ahem, Ashlee Simpson and Heidi Montag—you both looked perfectly fine before), it's silly and even downright dangerous to go under the knife just to tweak some disliked physical features. Rather than Botoxing and reconstructing every slightly imperfect feature, we need to learn how to simply highlight our *good* ones. And I know we all have at least one!

As much as we whine and complain about our ghetto booties and limp locks, we each have something we like about ourselves. Is it your Bette Davis eyes? The perfect-pout lips? How about those Celine Dion cheekbones? All-American girl Carrie Underwood has said, "I like my teeth. Sometimes I wonder if my orthodontist realizes how important he was." Whatever feature you feel good about, there is a way to bring it out even more.

Now that we've established our favorite area to underscore, we can learn to successfully play up that area with a few easy tricks and techniques—without spending ten grand to fix the things we aren't so crazy about.

The Eyes Have It! If you love your peepers and can't wait to play them up, read on for secret tips and tools for making them pop.

For blue or green eyes, pick up a brown eyeliner and a brown eyeshadow combination package—Revlon has a wonderful black/brown eyeliner to complement brown eyeshadow; both are really great and affordable. Or if you don't mind spending a little more, try Lorac's Croc Palette—not only is the shadow amazing, it comes in a fun little faux-crocodile palette that you'll never want to throw away. After prepping your skin with a good moisturizer (with SPF!), sweep on the lighter bronze color from your lash line to your eyelid crease, then blend the darker brown into the crease and just a bit above. For a nighttime look, add the eyeliner as close as possible to the lash line and blend the dark brown a bit deeper into the crease. Lightly brush a neutral shade from the base of the lashes to the brow bone. Finish with a couple of coats of good mascara—I recently started using Maybelline, and I thoroughly enjoy it.

If you're a brown-eyed girl, look for a deep gray or blue eyeliner and eyeshadow combination. My friend Megan has beautiful brown eyes, and she likes CoverGirl's semiliquid smoky gray and blue eyeliners. They also have a great brown-eye-enhancing color palette that works well with those liners. But if you're okay with shelling out a few more bucks, pick up a few smoky charcoal and pretty purple eye-lining pencils from Origins; they really do work and feel like magic, and it's all made with more skin-friendly substances! For daytime looks, brush on one of the lighter shades of gray and blue from your lash line to the crease. Then fill in the crease and a little above with the deepest color in the kit. To switch over to night, fill your lash line with the eyeliner and blend the dark blue and gray deeper into the crease. Sweep a shimmery, lighter shade from the base of the lashes to the brow bone. Finish off with a good mascara—if you want to splurge, try Guerlain's Le 2 de Guerlain Mascara.

If that's still not enough and you want to take your eyes even further, here are a few more not-so-secret-anymore top secrets!

- Origins has a great little product called Underwear for Lids, and it's practically divine. A couple of coats of this primer help your shadow and liner stay put hours longer. I heartily recommend it!
- If you're looking for a more dramatic eye effect, dip your eyeshadow applicator in water, shake off the excess, and apply the shadow as usual—the H_2O boost will deepen the shadow and create an even more smoldering effect.

👁 To create the appearance of even longer lashes, add an extra coat to the outer corners of both eyes.

Pucker Up! If you are crazy about your kisser and want to make those lips as alluring as possible, read on.

For a lighter complexion à la Sienna Miller or Reese Witherspoon, keep lips soft and neutral, so as not to overwhelm the rest of the face. Start with a lipliner pencil from Revlon or splurge on MAC's lovely-feeling Cremestick Liner. Carefully line the lips (nothing inside or outside the normal line—weird!) and then cover all over with a complimentary shade of lipstick—try something fiscally friendly from Rimmel's Rich Moisture Cream line or spring for NARS's amazing Belle de Jour Lipstick. Blend a dab of concealer in the center of the bottom lip and right under the center of your top lip for a little highlight, and then blot a light dusting of powder like Laura Mercier's Finishing Powder over the lips to seal in your hard work. Finish with a lighter-colored gloss from Lancôme's world-famous Juicy Tubes Smoothie lineup, or try one of Bobbi Brown's luxurious Glitter Lip Gloss sticks. Be prepared to get kissed!

For a darker complexion like America Ferrera or Leona Lewis, don't be afraid to go dark and dramatic on the lips. Start with a liner that is close to your natural lip color—Clinique has several beautiful dark shades in their Quickliner for Lips line, or go for broke with Benefit's Cupid's

Bow Lovely Lip Shaping Kit, which comes complete with the lip pencil, an applicator, and step-by-step instructions on how to fill in your lips correctly! Next find a great lipstick like Revlon's Just Bitten Lip Stain (it really does practically stain your lips: great for a long night out!) or Almay Lipcolor TLC (bonus: this one comes with clear gloss on the other end) and cover the entire area. Dab a bit of concealer in the center of the bottom lip and directly below the center of the top lip for a small touch of highlight, then seal everything with a setting powder like Cover FX's Translucent Setting Powder. To finish, add a swipe of really good lip gloss like NARS's Lipstain Gloss or Laura Mercier's Lip Glacé. They're pricey little items, but since we're not spending eight grand on plastic surgery, we might as well treat ourselves, right? And nothing feels quite as good as an expensive swipe of great makeup.

If you want to go the extra nine yards on your lips, here are a few trade secrets to stash away in your purse:

- If you need just a quick fix for your lips and don't have time to knock out the whole ten-minute routine, keep a tube of Bobbi Brown's Tinted Lip Balm on hand—it's a great moisturizer for your dried-out pucker and also provides a pick-me-up of color.
- If you still feel as if your lipstick lasts only about the duration of one *Bachelor* episode, try applying a few dol-

lops of liquid foundation to your lips before you slick on anything else, and then complete your normal makeup routine—it provides a solid base for the rest of the products.

👄 If you are dead set on having the longest-lasting shine *ever*, look into lip lacquer (that's right, not gloss—*lacquer*). MAC's Lipstick Lacquer is the best that I've found. It feels a little like Krazy Glue going on (and your boyfriend might refuse to kiss you), but you'll want to order it by the crateload after testing it out for a day or two.

Gettin' Cheeky with It If you have fabulous cheekbones, this is the section for you. Read on for simple ways to make them step up their game.

First of all, cheekbones are one of the more sun-exposed, freckle-prone areas of your body, thanks to the fact that they generally stick out just a bit farther than the rest of your facial features, so be sure and find a good daily moisturizer with at least SPF 15. (I have used Neutrogena's Summer Glow Daily Moisturizer SPF 15 for years—slather it on every day and you won't be sorry.) Second, my friend Emily introduced me to a great primer called Smashbox Photo Finish Foundation Primer—simply cover your entire face evenly and it will help keep everything in place for hours longer. Then apply the usual foundation, making sure to blend into the hairline and neck to avoid unwanted streaky lines and keep from looking like Jim Carrey in *The Mask*. If you aren't crazy about your usual foundation, try bareMinerals' SPF 15 Foundation—it's free of preservatives and chemicals that cause breakouts and comes in practically every shade under the sun.

For the next step, identify the top of your cheekbone and then apply the darkest shade of blush just below that. If you're looking for a sun-kissed daytime look, pick up one of Dior's luxurious Bronze Sunshine Blushes, or for a bright, peachy look try out a Lorac Cheek Stamp—they are equally fun to apply. To get a great nighttime look, try something a little darker from Laura Gellar's Blush-N-Brighten family (warning: it looks like a yummy, swirly dessert, and I almost ate it). After you've applied the darkest shade right below the top of your cheekbones, blend in a shimmery blush directly on top of your cheekbones; make sure it's something light and airy like Lancôme's Magique Mousse Blush—worth buying for the name alone. Blend it well and be sure to set those cheeks with a good finishing powder.

To get the cheekiest results, here are a few insider secrets:

♥ To find the ideal shade of blush, pick a hue that perfectly matches the color that your skin turns when you pinch your cheeks.

♥ Having trouble finding the right area to apply blush? Form a straight line with a pencil from the bottom of your nose to the point where the top of your ear meets your head. That line will indicate the top starting point for blush. And on the bottom, simply make sure that your blush never goes below the base of your nose.

♥ To create easy accentuation, pull your hair directly up and away from your face into a high ponytail—it instantly gives more definition to your cheekbones!

Another great way to look fabulous without overdoing it or cashing in birthday money for a nose job is to know what looks best on us. Audrey Hepburn once said, "There are certain shades of limelight that can wreck a girl's complexion." I'm sorry, no matter how much those weird, artsy ads may try to sell us shades of tangerine eyeshadow and tubes of turquoise mascara, I'm convinced that they flatter absolutely no one. Sure, it might be big on the runways this season, but when was the last time you saw one of those crazy get-ups on a real person out on the street? Never! It's the same thing with makeup. Dark nail polish is one thing, my friends, but lime green lip gloss is quite another. While perhaps trendy, extreme makeup is neither classy nor complimentary.

If you know that earth tones are your thing, then play around in that color group and create dozens of different looks that still *look good* on you. Do jewel tones look great with your skin? By all means, stock up and go crazy in that palette with shades that complement and flatter your lovely complexion. Just knowing what works with your skin tone will help avoid a plethora of cosmetic faux pas.

And finding that perfect color is easier than one might think, since everyone falls into one of two skin tone categories—warm or cool. For instance, I am a warm and am acutely aware that any sort of gray, purple, or navy blue looks pretty gross on me—and I'm okay with that. Those colors do absolutely nothing to complement my skin tone, and in fact, they make me appear even more pale and washed out than I already am—and Lord knows that's the last thing I need! So after lots of playing around with colors and products, I finally landed on a good palette that works with my warm skin tone. To find out what pigments and hues will best complement *your* skin tone, take the following warm/cool color challenge to find out your best possible makeup shades. Simply keep track of how many A's or B's you get:

HOT AND COLD

1. I receive the most compliments when I wear my:
    a. Red or orange shirt
    b. Blue or violet shirt
2. The skin in the crease behind my ear looks:
    a. Yellow
    b. Pink

3. When I look at the veins in my arm in natural light, they appear:
    a. Green
    b. Blue

4. If I hold a white piece of paper up to my face in bathroom vanity lighting after I shower, my skin looks:
    a. Yellow
    b. Blue

5. The type of jewelry I look best in is:
    a. Gold
    b. Silver

6. My natural hair color has:
    a. Reddish and gold undertones
    b. Bluish or ashy undertones

7. The wedding dress that would best complement me is:
    a. Ivory
    b. True white

If you have more A's than B's, you are probably a warm. Warms tend to have golden or apricot skin undertones and look great in gold jewelry. Your natural hair color may have flecks and highlights of red, gold, or yellow in it. Earth tones such as brown, cream, olive green, orange, mocha, and brick red look best on you. Look for makeup with copper, golden brown, beige, or ivory undertones—it will make your skin glow!

If you have more B's than A's, you are probably a cool. Cools tend to have pink or blue skin undertones and look stunning in silver jewelry. Your natural hair color may be pure black, brown, or ash blond. Jewel tones, such as emerald green and purple, look great on you, as do colors such as black and rosy pink. Look for makeup with yellow or pink undertones, such as icy pink, navy blue, and frosty shades of lilac, mauve, or charcoal—they will enhance your complexion and make your skin look radiant!

If you want to get really serious about your warm/cool composition, Prescriptives offers a complimentary skin-tone test at their counter that will identify your exact makeup needs. They can create customized blends of the foundation, powder, lips, bronzer, and concealer, that perfectly match your skin tone. How great is that?

It's fun to glam it up and pack on the shine, but every once in a while we need to give it a rest and just go au naturel. As nice as it is to look good, it's equally crucial to let our skin breathe after all that pore-clogging liquid foundation and caked-on concealer. You have to admit, nothing feels as good as clean skin fresh out of the shower, and every once in a while, we should just leave it that way!

If we don't have time to hose down at the end of the day, we can always cheat a little (I can't speak for your armpits—just your face) and use a great makeup remover. One of the best products I have found is Aveeno's Positively Radiant Daily

Cleansing Pads. (Technically, I guess you could wipe them under your pits if you really want/need to.) I'm personally a fan of the wipes, rather than the point-squirt-and-rinse bottle method that inevitably floods the bathroom and soaks my neck and shirt in drippy soap water, but that's just me. Somehow, it's just never quite as glamorous as when they splash it up on their faces in those Neutrogena commercials. The Aveeno wipes are hypoallergenic and seem to be very friendly to the skin. If you're particularly partial to the splash-'n'-go system, I recommend Kinerase Gentle Daily Cleanser. At $30 a pop it's a spendy little 6.6 ounces, but the green tea extracts make it worthwhile.

I'm all for just leaving our skin alone for a few hours, but I'm also abnormally paranoid about premature aging (blame it on the pasty-white freckled complexion that fries up like a sausage in the sun), so I always follow up cleansing with Oil of Olay's Age Defying Anti-Wrinkle Replenishing Night Cream. It's affordable and really does work like a charm. But, for a cheap, fun slumber-party-esque concoction for normal skin that's easy and effective, try whipping up your own night cream! Below is a quick one to try.

Cucumber Night Cream
½ *refrigerated cucumber, chopped with skin*
1 *egg white*
½ *cup olive oil*

1. Combine cucumber, egg white, and olive oil, and blend until smooth in a blender.

2. Apply mixture to the face, avoiding the eyes. Relax for about 20 minutes.

3. Remove with a dry cloth. Refrigerate any unused mixture, but try to use within a week.

Now you have fresh, glowing skin that looks absolutely radiant. You certainly do not *need* to wear makeup, but if and when you want to jazz things up a bit or even just look halfway presentable for work, you have the tools and resources to do so. There's no need to slather on a Vegas showgirl amount or try to keep up with the Kardashians; you can look flawless and gorgeous with minimal amounts of products used strategically. If we stick to highlighting our best features and relying on the right colors for our skin tone, we will look less like Bozo the Clown and more like Gwyneth Paltrow every single day. (Who am I kidding? Gwyneth Paltrow doesn't need a lick of makeup, ever!) I think the lovely and well-spoken Anne Hathaway put it all into perspective when she said, "I look my best after an entire hair and makeup team has spent hours perfecting me. When do I feel my best? When I haven't looked in a mirror for days, and I'm doing things that make me happy."

Chapter Eight

Have Your Cake and Eat It Too

"Let's face it, a nice creamy chocolate cake does a lot
for a lot of people; it does for me." —*Audrey Hepburn*

Believe it or not, curves used to be desirable. Busty?
Bring it on. Hippy? More to love! But thanks to the
South Beach Diet and constant promotion of size-2
models, we've been deluded into thinking that rail-thin
is the only form of beautiful. While the media merrily air-
brushes away unwanted butts and tummies and Mary-Kate
gets smaller by the day, we are stuck at home with an iden-
tity crisis: is it really okay to be a size 10? 14? 6? It's time that
we face off with our waistlines and be honest about models, the danger of obsession, dieting, and whether or not it's
possible to have dessert.

Famed chef Julia Child once said, "The only good time to
eat diet food is while you're waiting for the steak to cook."
Now, that's my kind of girl. But in our media-saturated

society, Eva Longoria's workout routine and Janet Jackson's diet are constantly being drilled into our heads. We get a meal-by-meal account of what Nicole Richie is up to these days, and know exactly what Jessica Simpson is eating to get back in shape. So even if you do have a decent self-image, it is nearly impossible to not get anxious or start obsessing about whether or not you're doing the right things with your body. Of course, the ironic thing is that those bodies that we place on a 'pedestal orbit around personal trainers and personal chefs. We could all look that great if the only thing we had to do all day was work on looking great! Unfortunately, most of us live in the real world and are lucky if we get to squeeze in an extra fifteen minutes on the elliptical at the gym.

Of course we still face a perfectly toned Gisele Bündchen on the billboard driving to work on Monday morning and a bronzed and beauteous sixty-foot Jessica Alba on the big screen on Friday night. Whether or not we like it, thin is in, and it's hard to escape that mentality. From Disney tween stars to yummy-mummy celebrities giving birth, we esteem the lean and beautiful and shake our heads at those who are tipping the scales. Though I'm not sure exactly when curvaceous physiques were declared unattractive and when the figure of a twelve-year-old boy became glamorous and appealing, it does appear that Skinny Minnie is here to stay. It's not surprising, though; between Jillian barking at her team members on *The Biggest Loser* and Kirstie Alley's weekly weigh-in on her *Fat Actress* show, it's no wonder we are constantly obsessing about our weight!

But when thoughts of eating and/or not eating start consuming our lives, it gets scary. We've all seen the horrors of eating disorders and may have even experienced some form of anorexia, bulimia, or binging ourselves. Between runway prototypes and red-carpet shots, the pressure to be thin is undoubtedly overwhelming. Many celebrities are affected by the pressure, as well, as evidenced by the vast number checking into rehab each year. I am certainly no doctor or psychiatrist but am unfortunately aware that the problem is beginning to affect younger and younger girls with every passing issue of *People*. A friend of mine has an eight-year-old daughter who recently asked to go on a diet! If not for our own well-being, we need to find a balance and healthy self-image for those who will come after us.

When we respect ourselves and our bodies, it shows. The gorgeously curvy America Ferrera says, "I feel like I'm a regular-size person . . . I know that having the perfect body doesn't fix all your problems, or make you love yourself more. To me, it's all about being comfortable in your own skin." Even the perfectly slender Kate Beckinsale has spoken up about the ideal body image, saying, "I don't think you can aspire to it, nor can I. Everybody is retouched, stretched, lengthened, slimmed, and trimmed. I could look at a picture of myself from the past and think, 'Why don't I look like that now?' It's because I never have."

I struggled with weight issues in high school, and it is a horrible issue to be consumed with. Being plagued day in and day out with thoughts of insecurity is no way to live life, and is indeed a sickness that takes months and, in many cases, years to recover from. The best way I found to counteract it was to accept myself for exactly who I was (even my meaty shoulders and arms!) and start celebrating the good parts, rather than focusing on the things I was unhappy with. I had to realize that I was made this way for a reason and that it was selfish and completely unrealistic to attempt to manipulate and distort my frame into a figure it clearly wasn't meant to be. Only when we are happy and at peace with ourselves can we begin to be a positive influence on those around us.

That is, of course, much easier said than done. Between the popularity of fad diets and high-demand gym memberships, body image can quickly become an obsession. We're constantly bombarded with fast-action weight-loss programs, miracle diet pills, low-fat menus, and preservative-packed boxed meals everywhere we go. We've got Chuck Norris busting a move on the pricey home gym system while Carmen Electra prances around in an aerobic striptease, but somehow these weight-loss solutions only seem to cause us more anxiety. So, rather than racing out to buy the latest workout contraption (which will inevitably either end up collecting dust in the basement or serving as a laundry rack), wrapping ourselves in seaweed for twenty-four hours, or living off maple syrup and cayenne pepper water for ten days, let's just start by making small, natural (not to mention rational) changes.

If you don't have two hundred bucks to drop on a detox day at the spa, you can try just drinking the recommended eight glasses of water a day. Instead of ordering the latest workout videos on Amazon, try going for a walk each night (which is also a great time to simply unwind, think, and recharge your batteries). Rather than investing in another bottle of fat-melting drugs, simply grab a piece of fruit for your four-o'clock sugar fix. There are many easy, classic ways to stop obsessing and start celebrating your shape, without depriving yourself of every semi-tasty scrap and crumb. The key is keeping a healthy balance.

It's no secret that it stinks to deprive yourself. When all you want is a piece of fudge ripple cake, it's out-and-out painful to instead force down a cardboard soy chip. When we deny ourselves for extended periods of time, we eventually hit a breaking point, go a little bit crazy, and raid our cupboards and takeout menus—manically pulling out every popcorn bag, pasta dish, and Snickers bar that we've so carefully avoided for months, and ordering up large pizzas, buckets of chicken, and cartons of fried rice. *That* is not healthy, either. You don't have to take part in the vicious cycle of yo-yo eating/dieting, though, if you balance everything. Guilty pleasures in moderation are 100 percent possible when you combine them with a steady diet of fruits, veggies, and other healthful eats.

Writer/producer/comedian Janette Barber has said, "When I buy cookies I eat just four and throw the rest away. But first I spray them with Raid so I won't dig them out of the garbage later. Be careful, though, because that Raid really doesn't taste that bad." We've probably all developed our little waistline strategies and intake idiosyncrasies, but the key is to simply not go overboard and refuse ourselves everything that we want for weeks on end. I'll be honest, I have fat-girl tendencies and could easily eat my body weight in stuffed-crust pizza. I can put away a pancake breakfast like it's nobody's business. But my body reacts about as well to a diet of processed cheese and white sugar as our sink did when I accidentally stuck a pair of scissors down the garbage disposal. So now I just eat those things in conjunction with a regular regimen of salads, fresh fruits, chicken, and the like. I don't know about you, but I think eating is enjoyable, and I'm not going to let a few highly publicized twigs keep me from having my cake and occasionally eating it, too!

Like I said before, I think we all have an inner indulger. I'd like to say that I've never entertained that side of my psyche, but I would be flat-out lying. As an ode to any food lover who has ever gluttonously partaken in an intake-frenzy fantasy, I composed a poem based on my undying affinity for a certain member of the dessert family. If you've ever downed an entire dish, platter, or serving, this one is for you!

Brownie

The guilty feeling that I probably should have had
was replaced by the thought that it wasn't that bad.
Although not even hungry, to that I'll confess,
I ponder what's wrong with having the rest.
Soon I have a rationalization
that nothing good can come from self-deprivation.
So polish it off! Heck, have the whole pan!
Soon I'm taken by the nine-by-thirteen quicksand.
First two, then three, then they start to fly—
the chocolate, the frosting—then four, then five.
I'm seven rows in and eight inches deep
when I pause for a moment to stop and breathe.
Then little by little, I start to slow down,
and closing my eyes, I curse the pounds
I'll undoubtedly gain from this calorie fest,
but I'm this far along, so why not the rest?!
Looking around, I see no one in sight,
and lifting my fork, I take the last bite.
Remorseful, triumphant, and pretty much sick,
I reflect on my deed and the empty dish.
Was it worth it? *I say to no one but me.*
At this rate you will never be a size three.
Who cares?! *I spout back.* It's not meant to be.
I'm a happy size eight who loves a good brownie.

I am convinced that we can happily and healthfully enjoy life to the fullest without cutting out every fry, steak, and cheesecake slice. One of the best ways to implement this old-fashioned sentiment is to (shocker!) develop a happy and healthy relationship with food. Rather than reducing it to boxed dinners and canned meal supplements, try balancing fresh, yummy things with the occasional slice of dessert. And instead of going on crazed, bizarre-o exercise kicks, try to take healthy measures in healthy doses, like walking or jogging with a friend several times a week. Pilates is my personal favorite and provides a great strengthening and toning workout while keeping you relaxed and improving your posture. Biking outdoors is also an extremely fun way to get in some physical activity and take in local sights that you might not usually see. And the time it takes to drag out your running shoes and go for a thirty-minute walk/run is completely worth it when you can stop by Baskin-Robbins for a cone afterward . . . since you burned all those calories! We can successfully stay cute and trim without sinking to bulimic measures or turning into hamsters on the workout wheel.

Here are a few quick ideas to stay healthy the old-fashioned way:

★ Turn snack breaks at work into walk breaks. Instead of loafing around the break room, get out and enjoy some fresh air, even if you only go around the block.

⭐ Take the stairs. Ten minutes of stair-walking can supposedly shave off up to 100 calories!

⭐ Rather than hitting up the movie theater again, suggest bowling or dancing for date night with your honey.

⭐ When stopping by the store, park as far away as possible and walk. This will also help to keep your doors from being dinged!

⭐ Walk your dog. If you don't have one, offer to walk your neighbor's—they will be extremely grateful. If it's a particularly cute dog, it might even be a guy magnet.

⭐ Offer to babysit for your boss. Heidi Klum says, "I also find that running around the house to keep up with three small children is a great workout in itself."

Another good way to keep up a healthy relationship with food is by cooking more. It's no secret that a steady diet of eating out is not the best way to implement portion control and calorie monitoring. We fly through the McDonald's drive-through, and the next thing we know we're left with nothing but a front seat full of Super-Sized-French-fry salt granules. How does that happen? I'm still not sure, but, we can avoid the fat-induced fest of eating out by simply eating in. Not only is a trip to the local farmer's market fun and interesting, it provides the freshest ingredients, as well as inspiration for future meals. Experiment with different cultures, cuisines, flavors, and spices. Invite friends over to help out, put on some music, and live it up. Some friends of mine actually have a weekly "family dinner night"; each week is a different theme (Mexican, Chinese, southern, etc.), and each member of the group of eight to ten friends brings over a side dish and pitches in to help the host with the main dish.

If you have a significant other, skip the pricey dinner plates at restaurants and spend a romantic evening in by grocery shopping for the night's menu together, preparing the meal with each other, and of course, doing the dishes together afterward. You'll most likely end up with leftovers, and they provide a great lunch to take to work the next day. You can also hone your freezer-friendly cooking skills by whipping up a few dishes for friends who have recently had a baby or are feeling under the weather—they will be eternally grateful to have an entire meal prepared for them. Another good way to have fun with food without gaining a bazillion pounds is by baking your favorite goodies on a Sunday night, saving one or two for yourself, then taking the rest to work on Monday morning for work peeps to enjoy (this is especially effective if there are a bunch of guys at your place of employment—if it's a female-dominated branch, those poor macaroons might sit there all day untouched if all the girls are on a diet). People will come out of the woodwork for baked goods, so you might even end up with a few new friends!

Making that food can be a whole other story, though. To

our premade-salad-and-Diet-Coke generation, the kitchen can be an intimidating place. But famed southern belle chef Paula Deen says, "It's nothing to be scared of, y'all. It's just food. . . . If it doesn't turn out, then just feed it to the dogs." I'm in love with her. Most of us probably grew up on Happy Meals and slowly graduated to Hot Pockets by college, so if you're like me and feel more like a microwave sous chef, don't feel bad. Between takeout, drive-through, and endless delivery options, it seems that good old-fashioned cooking has become a lost art. And to those who say cooking is merely an enslaving 1950s stereotype for women à la June Cleaver, I would argue that cooking is not merely a female burden dictated by society—it is a talent and a skill, and just like any craft or occupation, it requires practice, attention, preparation, and creativity. I have the utmost respect for people who know their way around the kitchen, and it's one of my goals in life to be able to create halfway edible meals for my own family.

A great way to celebrate food, friends, and proper etiquette is to throw an old-fashioned dinner party. Half the fun is just planning the menu, the decor, and the guest list! Stock up on Martha Stewart and Paula Deen magazines to get ideas for cooking, decorating, and planning, and don't forget to consult Emily Post for any etiquette questions. Overall, it's not as difficult as you might think to create a fun, classy evening for you and a few friends. Here is a quick to-do list to help you get started.

- 🍽 *Do* inform guests of dinner details. Let them know the expected attire, the menu, what to bring, and so forth ahead of time, via phone, e-vite, or snail mail.
- 🍽 *Do* craft a theme. Do red, white, and blue for the Fourth of July, break out your leaves and pumpkins for a fall fest, or go green for a St. Patrick's Day bash.
- 🍽 *Do* put guests at ease. Offer them a drink when they arrive, make sure there is enough seating for everyone, and see to it that each guest feels welcome and at home.
- 🍽 *Do* have a postdinner activity planned. Keep a group-friendly game on hand like Taboo or Catch Phrase, or rent several movies that could entertain the entire party.
- 🍽 *Do* send guests off with a little something. Make enough cupcakes for everyone to take one home, stash cellophane to-go bags with small candies, or keep a basket of chocolates by the door for guests to take as they leave.

Besides being inventive, satisfying, and possibly even therapeutic, cooking is a great way to develop a healthy relationship with food. It not only tests your self-control—Will I single-handedly polish off the whole batch of dough before it makes it to cookie form—you'll also appreciate the final product more after you've put in your own blood, sweat, and tears (hopefully not literally—yeek).

I've heard it said that food is such a foundational part of

our lives that often the mere sharing of recipes with strangers turns them into good friends. So if you've made it this far into the book, first of all, I'm impressed. Second, I'd like to think that we are more than just strangers by now. So to solidify our newfound friendship and jump-start our new healthy relationship with food and cooking, I've included a few of my favorite recipes for you to try (I would love to hear yours, as well!). Some of these are good for you, while others have more carbs than an elephant sandwich. But they're all quite tasty, if I do say so myself, and should absolutely be shared with others. So, with Paula's philosophy in mind, let's try cooking something!

The first is my husband's salsa recipe. Drew's mom (who could seriously give Martha Stewart a run for her domestic-skills money) imparted all of her kitchen-savvy and flavor know-how to him and his sister, so when he's not doing boy things like growing a beard or lighting the grill, he loves to cook. And, like any sane woman, I let him! This beautiful appetizer/snack may be addictive, but the good thing is that it consists purely of healthy, good-for-you ingredients. So feel free to snarf down the whole bowl by yourself.

Drew's Salsa

3 cups fresh tomatoes, seeded and diced

1 cup fresh green onions, diced

1 cup fresh cilantro, finely chopped

1 tablespoon fresh garlic, chopped

1¼ teaspoon salt
1 teaspoon cumin
½ teaspoon chili powder
¼ teaspoon black pepper
1¼ teaspoons lime juice
½ teaspoon lemon juice
Multigrain tortilla chips

1. Mix together tomatoes, onions, cilantro, and garlic in a large bowl.

2. Combine salt, cumin, chili powder, and black pepper in a smaller bowl, then add to tomato mixture.

3. Stir in lime and lemon juice. Mix until all ingredients are combined.

4. Cover and refrigerate until ready to eat. Serve with multigrain tortilla chips and enjoy!

Makes 6 cups.

If I had to choose my last meal on earth, it would be a full-blown breakfast. We're talking eggs, buttermilk pancakes, chocolate milk—the works. Consequently, Drew and I used to frequent the neighborhood Waffle House almost daily and were even on a first-name basis with Kathy, the night-shift waitress. Due to my sick obsession with pre-noon foods, I feel compelled to share my favorite breakfast recipe with you: French toast. Seriously, what red-blooded creature can resist

the combination of maple syrup, powdered sugar, and bread?
Not me! So, without further ado, here is my beloved method
for French toast—and I'm not above serving it for dinner.

Tennessee French Toast

½ pint fresh strawberries, hulled and sliced

2 tablespoons sugar, divided

6 extra-large eggs

1½ cups half-and-half

2 tablespoons honey

2 teaspoons pure vanilla extract

1 teaspoon salt

1 loaf of brioche

Salted butter

Vegetable oil

Confectioners' sugar

Maple syrup (optional)

1. Combine the fresh strawberries and 1 tablespoon of sugar in a small bowl and set aside.

2. In a large bowl, whisk together eggs, half-and-
half, honey, 1 tablespoon of sugar, vanilla, and salt.

3. Slice the brioche loaf into three-fourths-inch
slices and soak 1 or 2 slices in the egg mixture for
approximately five minutes, turning once.

4. Heat 1 teaspoon of butter and 1 teaspoon of

oil in a large sauté pan over medium heat. Remove a slice of bread from the egg mixture and cook for 2 to 3 minutes on each side. Soak additional bread slices in the egg mixture while you're waiting for each batch to cook. Continue to add butter and oil to the pan as needed.

5. Sprinkle finished slices with confectioners' sugar and top with strawberries. Serve with maple syrup or additional honey.

Serves 6 to 8.

Let's be honest, this just wouldn't be a good book if it was void of a dessert recipe. And since we've got a female-bonding-ya-ya-traveling-pants-sisterhood thing going on here, I think it needs to be a chocolate one. One of my absolute favorite desserts to make is these unbelievable German chocolate bars—I'm serious, they will change your life. These gooey morsels of chocolately goodness will have every girlfriend cursing her diet and every guy within a four-mile radius eating out of your hand. They are very simple to make and, just for the record, definitely fall under that not-so-healthy category. But once you have one, you won't care!

Gooey German Chocolate Bars
1 package German chocolate cake mix
½ cup (1 stick) butter, softened

1 tub pecan coconut frosting
¾ bag semisweet chocolate chips
½ cup whole milk
Vanilla bean ice cream (optional)

1. Preheat oven to 350 degrees and grease a 9 × 13-inch pan.

2. Pour cake mix into a large mixing bowl. Cut softened butter into cake mix using a pastry blender or by crisscrossing two knives.

3. Press exactly half of the mixture into the bottom of the greased 9 × 13-inch pan. Bake for 10 minutes.

4. Remove pan from oven and carefully spread pecan coconut frosting over the baked layer. Evenly sprinkle chocolate chips over the layer of frosting.

5. In a separate bowl, combine milk and remaining cake mixture. Do not overmix. Drop by teaspoonfuls onto the layer of chocolate chips.

6. Bake for 23 to 28 minutes. Let cool completely (two hours at the very least, overnight is preferred). Cut into squares and serve as individual bars or with a scoop of vanilla bean ice cream.

Makes 15 bars.

Since we're on the subject of dessert, I think we need to start actually ordering it at restaurants. Life is too short to pass up the dessert cart! I'm officially over the wan "Oh, I'm really too full, I couldn't eat another bite" facade that we girls assume on dates and social outings. We feign a polite, stuffed expression while secretly waiting for someone else in the party to speak up for the crème brûlée or fudgy peanut butter bomb, while we are stuck furtively eyeing the after-dinner menu, salivating over the dessert cart, and inevitably fantasizing about that left-behind piece of mousse pie for the rest of the day. So if you're not on a job interview or dining with a dignitary from another culture where dessert is offensive, speak up for that last piece of lava cake! You know that everyone else at the table wants it, too, so be an inspiration and start a chain reaction of post-lunch goodness.

Likewise, one of the best ways to keep from overdoing it in those kinds of situations is to have an occasional reward, so that when we get around a family-style banana split we don't eat the entire family's portion ourselves! My friend Erica used to keep a stash of Dove chocolates in her locker at work and allowed herself to have one every day. My aunt Connie buys individual servings of Laughing Cow cheese to help with portion control. And my mom is famous for the "candy stash" that she keeps in her purse (note: purse-contained candy stashes should consist of nonmelty items like hard butterscotch candies and Life Savers; otherwise, after an hour in the car, said purse will look like a Willy

Wonka Chocolate Factory branch at the threshold of Hades). I keep a package of Riesen in my desk drawer—the key is simply not to eat your stash all at once.

So what is your guilty pleasure? Thai takeout? Schedule a monthly stop at International Cuisine and enjoy those veggie eggrolls and pad Thai noodles. Love popcorn? Keep an air popper handy and make a semihealthy treat to munch on during movie night. Can't get enough hot dogs? Try—okay, I can't bring myself to say anything nice about them. They are compressed tubes of ground-up hooves and teeth. But my family loves them, and I suppose millions of other people do, as well, so if hot dogs are your thing, splurge on those processed nitrate links at the baseball game and go crazy.

Can you really have your cake and eat it, too? Absolutely. We need to stop letting Hollywood dictate our diets and start finding a healthy balance that is right for us. Even the beautiful and refreshingly normal Mandy Moore says, "I'm *much* happier to present this type of person. I'm not Nicole Richie. I'm not like a toothpick, and I will never be. I'm just a regular-looking person—and that's okay. It's taken a while to come to grips with that since it's definitely not the norm in my business. But, like, who cares? If anything, that makes someone more special—or at least that's what I tell myself." Not all of us are cut out to be a single-digit pants size, and we need to realize that a 12 can be just as beautiful as a 2. You can healthfully and happily maintain your weight without taking any weird voodoo pills or sprinting a marathon on the treadmill every week. You simply need to find a steady balance between those leafy greens and that Sprinkles cupcake. Let's become the new poster children for happy, healthy young women.

Finally, another great way to combine food and fun is by helping others. Audrey was a great example of this: as a goodwill ambassador to UNICEF, she spent decades of her life bringing aid and relief to impoverished children in some of the most remote locations of the world. World Vision is another amazing organization—every year they send out "Christmas catalogs," giving us the opportunity to send someone in a developing country a chicken or goat for Christmas so that they can have fresh eggs, milk, or cheese every day! Helping others with food doesn't need to cost us a dime, though. Just by volunteering to serve meals at a local homeless shelter or offering a hand behind the scenes at a soup kitchen, we can touch countless people's lives. Sharing food with someone can break down language barriers, racial stereotypes, and social walls, as well as keep us from taking our own blessings for granted. Food is a natural gatherer of people, and we should embrace that!

Now What?

"It is better to light one small candle than to curse
the darkness." —*Eleanor Roosevelt*

I'm pretty sure that Jane Austen has already rolled over in her grave by now, but I like to think that we can be the ones to put her back. It's the least we can do for all the dignified and classy ladies who have gone before us and paved the way for greatness: Audrey Hepburn, Florence Nightingale, heck, even our grandmothers! Rather than sitting back and watching as our generation gets swallowed up by Juicy Couture and MTV, let's step up and take back our dignity. Our culture is in desperate need of real women with brains, beauty, and self-respect—women who aren't afraid to take risks, dream big, and order dessert. If we don't do it, who will?

Clearly, we can't rely on the girls splashed across Page Six to hold up our feminine honor and reputation. In fact, rather than upholding any kind of proud legacy or time-honored glory, they're driving our good name into the ground! We've got a lot to uphold—and a lot to lose. For decades, young ladies like ourselves sweated, toiled, and gave up years of their lives so that we could have a voice. They wrote, fought, challenged, petitioned, and went against social protocol to obtain the liberties we have now, and I hate to see those values just circling the drain. That's why I am willing to work for the rest of my life to build a positive reputation and am thrilled that you've decided to join me! Hermès scarves, cute boys, chocolate cake . . . none of them will matter after we're gone—but we *can* leave behind a legacy, one that our mothers would be proud of and our own daughters will be inspired by.

If our own reputations weren't reason enough to ditch the Stupid act, we have living, breathing incentive that provides even more ammunition for us to turn in our glitter eyeshadow and plastic tiaras—the generation of girls coming after us. While most of us grew up in a blissfully naive world of *Saved by the Bell* and My Little Pony, our daughters and nieces are going to have to contend with *Girls Gone Wild* and Bratz dolls. While we were lucky enough to have at least a few positive role models like Niki Taylor, Princess Diana, and Oprah, their affirmative and inspiring celebrities are largely overshadowed by the car-crashing, pot-smoking, crotch-baring kind that have sunk to new lows, even for Hollywood.

While my parents took us to Sunday school and taught us the value of manners, responsibility, and modesty, I can't help but worry that our own children will grow up devoid of moral priorities and normal-length skirts, with nothing more than the enticement to flash their hooters to some sicko in a trailer on spring break, go pole dancing in a barely-there bikini, and conveniently forget underwear when they leave the house, all accompanied by a sense of entitlement that allows them to wear Juicy sweatsuits 24/7 and avoid any kind of real work. To provide evidence that this really is happening out there, my husband and I went out to eat the other night and our waiter began telling us "cute" stories of how his *three-year-old* daughter gives people the bird while they're driving and recently learned the f-word. Besides being appalled and horrified, I was heartbroken. That poor girl has almost no chance at becoming a woman of class and dignity. Why? Because no one is there to provide a good example! Our waiter informed us that he and his ex-wife don't attempt to teach her any different, and I'm all too aware that anything she sees on TV will only further encourage her pint-sized Stupid Girl behavior. We have a responsibility to the next generation; if we don't work to change the current classless, skanky, dim-witted trend, no one will.

I'm not 100 percent sure, but I suspect you and I are a lot alike. I'm guessing that you, like myself, would like to leave behind something we can be proud of: a feminine legacy of hard work, self-respect, style, success, class, and grace—a fulfilled life that our mothers would be proud of and our own daughters wouldn't be ashamed of. That legacy, of course, will be different for each of us. As sassy, unique individuals, we each have inherent virtues and values we would like to instill in those who come after us. Some of us may want to pass on a reputation of strength and courage; others may want to infuse a sense of poise and dignity. Some may hope to leave a heritage of style and class, and others will want to let our daughters know that they inherited a legacy of wisdom and faith. No matter what positive traits we value, keeping them alive is crucial to overcoming the Stupid Girl culture. Because after all the bars have closed, the Abercrombie sales have ended, and our numerous love interests have disappeared, we'll be left with just our legacy and reputations (and possibly a kid or two!).

The art of living with style, class, and grace is clearly not the trend in Hollywood, and said lifestyle doesn't seem to be a big priority in real life anymore, either. Sure, it might be easier to say yes and spend the night clubbing, but staying home to study for the GRE could get you into Harvard. It would probably be easier to buy the see-through

V-neck that lets your boobs hang out, but finding the three-quarter-sleeve button up might get you the corporate job you've been after. It also might be easier to text your crush and let him know your true feelings, but leaving him wanting more might get you that second date. So, the chic, intelligent way might not be the easy way, but since when was anything worth doing easy?

Old-fashioned values and ideals are not necessarily a bad thing. In fact, I think our modern-girl world could use a lot more of them. The polite manners, proper etiquette, and refined language that our great-grandmothers were raised on could be a much-needed splash of cold water on today's dumbed-down reality world. The chic dress, sophisticated style, and thoughtful modesty of Audrey's era could be a saving grace for our teensy-weensy shirts-'n'-skirts age. Selfless sacrifices for friends, demure dating decorum, and healthy outlooks on dessert could come in handy when navigating our current world of tacky excess. Thankfully, these are not lost arts . . . yet. They've simply been pushed aside for a while. We need to act now before they become eternally extinct. I love what Eleanor Roosevelt said about lighting one small candle rather than cursing the darkness. The truth is, it's easy to sit around and criticize Paris, Britney, and Lindsay all day, but until we get out and make a change ourselves, complaining won't do us, or anyone else, a bit of good. So rather than stop at blaming, let's go beyond what's comfortable and light our small candles. Once we've got that classy glow about us, others will be naturally attracted to it. We can be the ones to bring back virtue, discretion, and elegance and permanently reintroduce the art of living with style, class, and grace.

Thank You!

Lord, You are so good. You have given me more than I deserve and more than I could have ever hoped for. Drew, you are the funniest man I know and I'm so glad you asked me out. If I am a goofus on the roofus hollering my head off, you are one too! Paisley, thank you for keeping me company while I wrote this book. You are the love of my life and have brought me more joy than you'll ever know. Mom, I could never, ever, *ever* begin to say how much I love and appreciate you. I can say with complete certainty that you are the most fun mother to ever walk the planet, and I'm so proud to be your daughter. Abby, I could fill an entire book with inside jokes and quotes between the two of us, but for now I will just say that you are so much more than a sister to me; you are a best friend. Mark, Patti, and Hannah, you are the best in-laws a girl could ask for. Thank you for your continuous love, generosity, and technical assistance. ☺ Caren, thank you for believing in this book from the very beginning. You deserve a gold medal for all the work you put into this. And, finally, a big thank you to everyone at Hachette Book Group—I feel incredibly privileged to be part of your family.

About the Author

JORDAN CHRISTY is a publicist for Warner Bros. Records and has worked with many artists, celebrities, and media outlets. She has also written for various fashion magazines and music trade publications. Jordan lives in Nashville, Tennessee, with her husband, Drew, and their beautiful baby girl, Paisley.